U.S. Chemical Safety and Hazard Investigation Board

I0488464

INVESTIGATION REPORT

DUST EXPLOSION

(6 Killed, 38 Injured)

WEST PHARMACEUTICAL SERVICES, INC.

KINSTON, NORTH CAROLINA
JANUARY 29, 2003

KEY ISSUES

HAZARD RECOGNITION AND COMMUNICATION
GOOD ENGINEERING PRACTICE
LOCAL AMENDMENTS TO FIRE CODES

REPORT NO. 2003-07-I-NC
SEPTEMBER 2004

Abstract

This investigation report examines a dust explosion at West Pharmaceuticals, Inc., in Kinston, North Carolina. Six workers were killed and 38 others were injured, including two firefighters. The Kinston plant manufactured rubber drug-delivery components. This report identifies the root and contributing causes of the incident and makes recommendations on hazard recognition and communication, good engineering practice, and local amendments to fire codes.

The U.S. Chemical Safety and Hazard Investigation Board (CSB) is an independent Federal agency whose mission is to ensure the safety of workers, the public, and the environment by investigating and preventing chemical incidents. CSB is a scientific investigative organization; it is not an enforcement or regulatory body. Established by the Clean Air Act Amendments of 1990, CSB is responsible for determining the root and contributing causes of accidents, issuing safety recommendations, studying chemical safety issues, and evaluating the effectiveness of other government agencies involved in chemical safety.

No part of the conclusions, findings, or recommendations of CSB relating to any chemical incident may be admitted as evidence or used in any action or suit for damages arising out of any matter mentioned in an investigation report (see 42 U.S.C. § 7412 [r][6][G]). CSB makes public its actions and decisions through investigation reports, hazard investigations, safety recommendations, case studies, safety bulletins, incident digests, special technical publications, and statistical reviews. More information about CSB may be found at www.csb.gov.

CSB publications may be downloaded at www.csb.gov or obtained by contacting:

U.S. Chemical Safety and
Hazard Investigation Board
2175 K Street NW, Suite 400
Washington, DC 20037-1848
(202) 261-7600

CSB investigation reports may be purchased from:

National Technical
Information Service
5285 Port Royal Road
Springfield, VA 22161-0002
(800) 553-NTIS or
(703) 487-4600
Email: info@ntis.fedworld.gov

For international orders, see:
www.ntis.gov/support/
cooperat.htm.

For this report, refer to NTIS
number PB2005-100005

Contents

Contents (cont'd)

Figures and Table

Figures

Table

Acronyms and Abbreviations

AC	Alternating current
ACS	Automated rubber compounding system
ASTM	American Society for Testing and Materials
ATF	Bureau of Alcohol, Tobacco, Firearms and Explosives
ATSDR	Agency for Toxic Substances and Disease Registry
bar-m/sec	Bar-meter per second
CFD	Computational fluid dynamics
CFR	Code of Federal Regulations
CMU	Concrete masonry unit
CSB	U.S. Chemical Safety and Hazard Investigation Board
EMS	Emergency Medical Services Division, Lenoir County Department of Emergency Services
EPA	U.S. Environmental Protection Agency
ERM	Environmental Resources Management
°F	Degrees Fahrenheit
FDA	U.S. Food and Drug Administration
FMEA	Failure modes and effects analysis
HazCom	Hazard Communication Standard (OSHA)
HSE	Health and Safety Executive, United Kingdom
HVAC	Heating, ventilating, and air conditioning
ICC	International Code Council
IFC	International Fire Code
LEV	Local exhaust ventilation
LTA	Less than adequate
m^3	Cubic meter
mJ	Millijoule
MIE	Minimum ignition energy

MOU	Memorandum of understanding
Namico	National Milling & Chemical Co., Inc.
NCDENR	North Carolina Department of Environment and Natural Resources
NCDOL	North Carolina Department of Labor
NCOSHA	Occupational Safety and Health Division (NCDOL)
NEC	National Electric Code
NFPA	National Fire Protection Association
NMR	New materials review
OSHA	Occupational Safety and Health Administration
psi	Pounds per square inch
psig	Pounds per square inch gage
SCE	Safety Consulting Engineers, Inc.

A January 29, 2003, dust explosion at the West Pharmaceutical Services, Inc., plant in Kinston, North Carolina, killed six workers and injured 38 others, including two firefighters.

The Kinston facility manufactured rubber drug-delivery components such as syringe plungers, septums, and vial seals. Production operations included rubber compounding, molding, and extrusion. The rubber compounding process consisted of two separate production lines, each with a mixer, a mill, and batchoff equipment. Raw materials were prepared in another area of the plant.

The U.S. Chemical Safety and Hazard Investigation Board (CSB) determined that accumulated polyethylene dust above a suspended ceiling fueled the explosion. Because of the extent of damage to the Kinston facility, it was not possible to definitively determine the event that dispersed the dust or what ignited it.

CSB determined the following root causes of the January 29 incident:

- West did not perform adequate engineering assessment of the use of powdered zinc stearate and polyethylene as antitack agents in the rubber batchoff process.

- West engineering management systems did not ensure that relevant industrial fire safety standards were consulted.

- West management systems for reviewing material safety data sheets did not identify combustible dust hazards.

- The Kinston plant's hazard communication program did not identify combustible dust hazards or make the workforce aware of such.

CSB makes substantive recommendations to West Pharmaceutical Services, Inc., to:

- Develop/revise policies and procedures for new material safety reviews, and safety reviews of engineering projects.

- Ensure that its manufacturing facilities that generate combustible dusts meet the requirements of National Fire Protection Association (NFPA) Standard 654.

- Improve hazard communication programs.

CSB recommends to the North Carolina Building Code Council that the State fire code be amended to require compliance with NFPA 654. Additionally, recommendations are made to the North Carolina Department of Labor, Occupational Safety and Health Division; North Carolina Code Officials Qualification Board; and Crystal, Inc.–PMC.

1.0 Introduction

1.1 Background

On Wednesday, January 29, 2003, at 1:28 pm, an explosion and fire at the West Pharmaceutical Services, Inc., plant in Kinston, North Carolina, killed six workers and injured at least 38 others, including two responding firefighters. Much of the facility—which manufactured small rubber parts for pharmaceutical delivery devices—was severely damaged.

One student was injured when windows were broken at a school 0.7 mile away. Businesses located in the same industrial park as West were damaged, and windborne burning debris ignited fires in wooded areas as far as 2 miles away. One home located nearby was damaged slightly, and at least two families were evacuated as a precautionary measure.

Because of the number of deaths and injuries, the U.S. Chemical Safety and Hazard Investigation Board (CSB) launched an investigation to determine the root and contributing causes of the explosion and to make recommendations to prevent similar occurrences.

. . . An explosion and fire . . . killed six workers and injured at least 38 others, including two responding firefighters.

1.2 Investigative Process

The Lenoir County Department of Emergency Services[1] commanded the incident response. Officers of the Lenoir County Sheriff's Department controlled site access and security. CSB investigators arrived at the site on the evening of January 29. CSB investigators and agents from the Bureau of Alcohol, Tobacco, Firearms and Explosives (ATF) worked under the terms of an existing Memorandum of Understanding (MOU) and entered the site jointly after unstable portions of the plant were secured and made safe for entry. CSB also worked under MOUs with the U.S. Environmental Protection Agency (EPA) and the Agency for Toxic Substances and Disease Registry (ATSDR).

EPA and the North Carolina Department of Environment and Natural Resources (NCDENR) performed air monitoring and screening of water runoff from the firefighting effort. West

---

[1]This County department includes an Emergency Management Division and an Emergency Medical Services (EMS) Division, among others.

contracted with HEPACO, Inc., an environmental cleanup company, and with Environmental Resources Management (ERM) to set up a water treatment and filtration system to reduce the discharge of potential chemical contaminants into the environment.

The North Carolina State Bureau of Investigation assisted ATF with interviews. Intentional criminal activity was ruled out, and ATF concluded that the explosion was accidental. In such circumstances, the MOU calls for ATF to forgo further analysis and for CSB to continue the investigation. In addition, inspectors from the North Carolina Department of Labor (NCDOL), Occupational Safety and Health Division (NCOSHA), and the U.S. Occupational Safety and Health Administration (OSHA) remained on scene to conduct a separate investigation.

CSB began interviewing hourly and contract workers, as well as plant management personnel, on the morning after the incident. In addition, CSB:

- Examined damage to the facility and reviewed design plans and documents.

- Commissioned testing of product ingredients and other materials found throughout the plant.

- Reviewed pertinent codes, standards, technical guidelines, management practices, and regulations.

1.3   West Corporate Profile

West is one of the world's largest manufacturers of closures and components for sealing drug vials and prefilled syringes.

West is one of the world's largest manufacturers of closures and components for sealing drug vials and prefilled syringes. Headquartered in Lionville, Pennsylvania, the company has approximately 4,000 employees working in eight facilities in North America and 10 in Europe and Asia. West was founded in 1923 and is publicly traded. In 2003, sales exceeded $490 million (West, 2004).

1.4 Kinston Facility

West's Kinston facility has manufactured drug-delivery components—such as syringe plungers, septums, and vial seals—since 1975. The rubber compounding process in use at the time of the incident started up in 1987, following a major expansion and automation project. At the time of the incident, 264 West employees and 35 full-time contract workers were employed at the plant.

The rubber compounding process at the Kinston plant was generally similar to other rubber manufacturing processes, such as tire production. It was semicontinuous, producing sequential batches and operating 24 hours per day, 5 or 6 days per week.

1.5 Facility Overview

The West plant was located in a light industrial business park adjacent to the regional airport. Two private residences and the local Humane Society shelter were each located about 1,000 feet from the facility. The plant was approximately 150,000 square feet in area and primarily single story; however, some of the rubber compounding equipment was located on a 60.5-foot-high second floor area (Figure 1). The plant housed two operations—rubber compounding and finishing, in which the compounded rubber was molded and pressed into stoppers and plungers.

The plant housed two operations—rubber compounding and finishing . . .

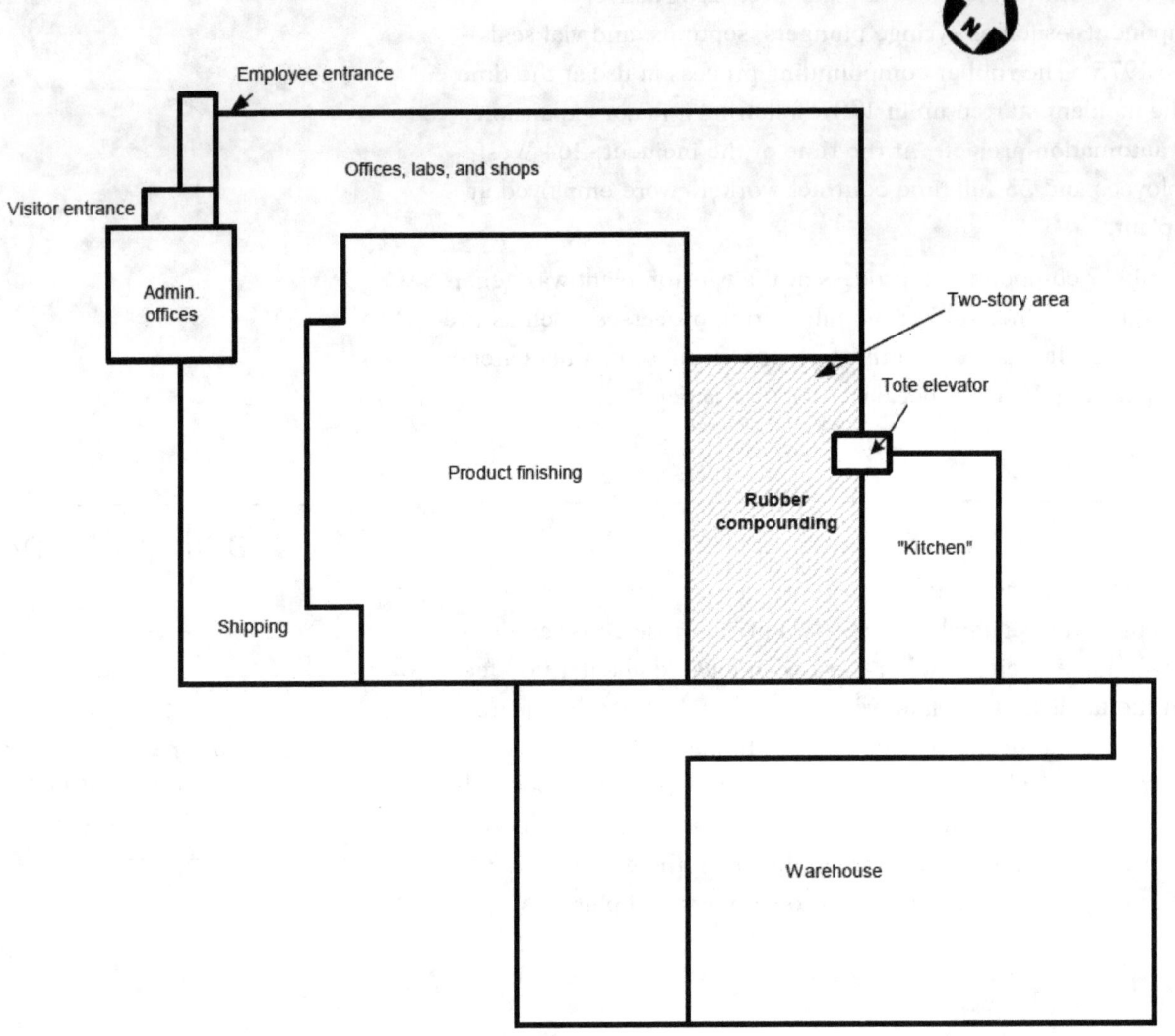

Figure 1. Layout of West Pharmaceutical Services Kinston facility.

1.6.1 Overview

The automated rubber compounding system (ACS) consisted of two separate production lines, each with a mixer, a mill, and batchoff[2] equipment. Raw materials were prepared in the "kitchen"—a separate section of the plant. Solid materials were weighed in the kitchen and loaded into totes. A roller conveyor transported the totes to an elevator, where they were lifted to the second floor of the compounding structure. A conveyor then carried the totes to the mixers, where the ingredients were compounded. Other solid ingredients used in large quantities, such as clay, were pneumatically conveyed through pipes to the second-floor mixers. Liquid mineral oil used as a plasticizer[3] for the rubber blends was piped directly to the mixers.

Once compounded in the mixers, the rubber dropped through chutes to the ground floor, where roller mills smoothed it into strips. The strips of rubber were trimmed, dipped into a vat containing a slurry of very fine polyethylene powder and water, and then air dried and stacked for shipment or molding in the finishing area of the plant.

A suspended acoustic tile ceiling hung 10.5 feet above floor level. The ceiling covered the entire room where the rubber was rolled, dipped, cooled, and folded (Figure 2).

Once compounded in the mixers, the rubber dropped through chutes to the ground floor, where roller mills smoothed it into strips.

A suspended acoustic tile ceiling hung 10.5 feet above floor level. The ceiling covered the entire room where the rubber was rolled, dipped, cooled, and folded.

---

[2]"Batchoff" is a term of art used in the rubber processing industry. Rubber is compounded in batches. The batchoff machine cools, coats, and folds the strips of rubber from a compounded batch.

[3]A plasticizer is a substance that—when blended with plastic or rubber—increases the flexibility of the material.

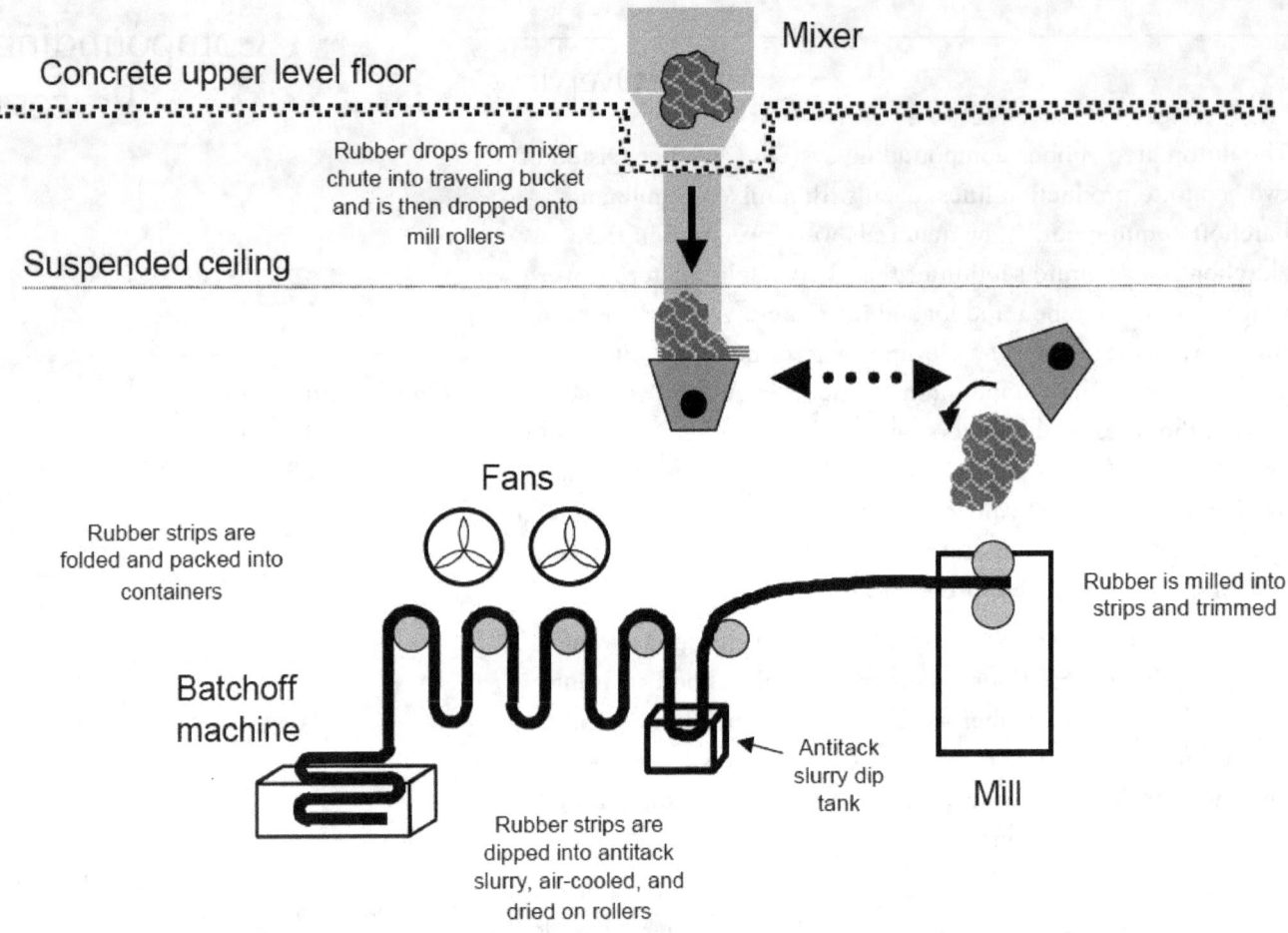

Figure 2. Simplified two-story rubber compounding process diagram.

1.6.2 Kitchen

Bulk materials, such as raw rubber or synthetic polymers, were cut and weighed on one side of the kitchen; employees used the other side for measuring powders.

The kitchen was a process area located east of the rubber compounding area and separated from it by a concrete masonry firewall. Bulk materials, such as raw rubber or synthetic polymers, were cut and weighed on one side of the kitchen; employees used the other side for measuring powders. An automatic carousel dispensed smaller-portion ingredients. Roller conveyors along each side of the kitchen moved the totes with premeasured components to an elevator in the northwest corner of the room

(Figure 3); the totes were then sent to either of two mixers located on the second floor.

As a quality control procedure, each tote was individually barcoded—as was each separately bagged component in the tote. The mixer operator checked the barcodes to verify components before loading the contents into the mixer.

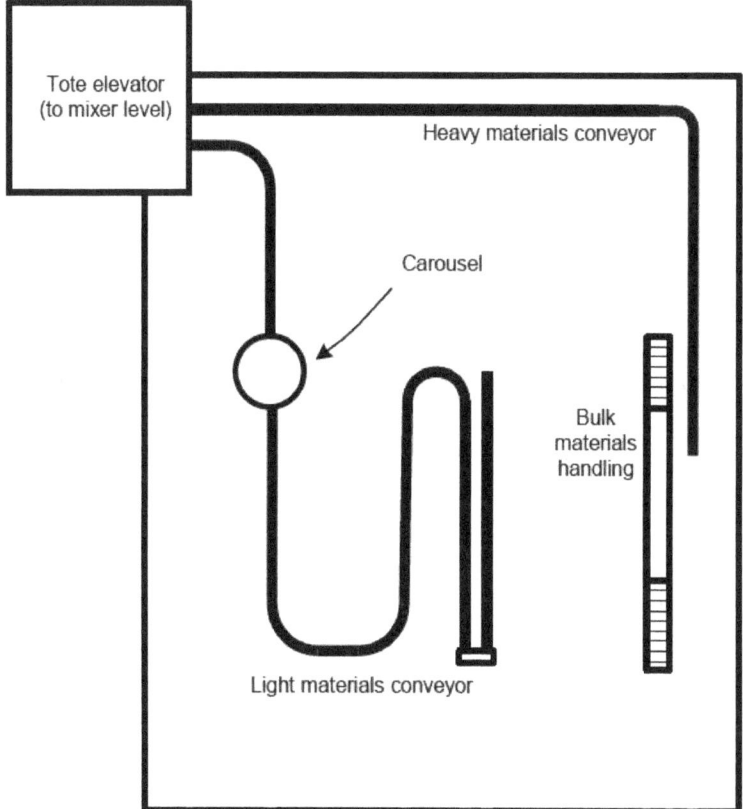

Figure 3. Plan sketch (view from above) of kitchen layout.

1.6.3 Mixing

Automatic controls hold the process temperature below the onset for vulcanization.

The rubber mixers[4] were located in recessed areas on the upper level of the compounding structure. Ingredients were generally loaded into the mixers through an open hatch on the side.

However, bulk powders used in large portions—such as calcined clay—were pneumatically transferred to weigh hoppers and automatically dropped into the mixers. After the batch was loaded, the operator closed the feed door and engaged the automatic controls.

The kneading action of the mixer causes frictional heating of the rubber. Although chilled cooling water flows through the machine's kneading rotors, the varying speed of the rotors and the duration of the mixing phase largely control the temperature of the rubber. Automatic controls hold the process temperature below the onset for vulcanization.[5] The rubber is vulcanized later during the forming process, when the finished products are molded.

When the batch reaches a predefined temperature or time limit . . . the rubber [drops] through a chute into a bucket located in the mill area on the ground floor.

When the batch reaches a predefined temperature or time limit, the automatic controls open a door on the bottom of the mixer to allow the rubber to drop through a chute into a bucket located in the mill area on the ground floor.

1.6.4 Milling

The flattened rubber is cut into a strip, which then enters another machine—referred to as the "batchoff"—where it is cooled, coated, and folded.

The rubber is dumped from the bucket onto the milling machine, where steel rollers cool, flatten, and smooth it into a sheet of roughly uniform thickness. The flattened rubber is cut into a strip, which then enters another machine—referred to as the "batchoff"—where it is cooled, coated, and folded.

---

[4]Each mixer has two opposing rotors that mesh, pull, and shear the rubber components to create a uniform mix; the process is aided by the frictional heat generated by the mixer.

[5]"Vulcanization" refers to the process of heating rubber in the presence of sulfur or other agents to form crosslinks between the rubber molecules, which gives the rubber greater elasticity and strength.

1.6.5 Cooling, Coating, and Folding

In the batchoff machine, the rubber strip first passes through a dip tank containing a slurry of polyethylene powder and water.[6] The powder is very fine, with an average particle size of 12 microns, and acts as an antitack agent.[7] The water slurry further cools the rubber so that retained heat does not promote premature vulcanization.

After leaving the dip tank, the rubber is passed in front of a series of air fans. The fans draw air from the room and blow it across the rubber strip, drying it as water evaporates from the surface. At the exit of the batchoff, the rubber is folded and packed in containers. It is then stored prior to use in the molding section of the plant or shipped to another West facility.

Almost all of the powdered antitack ingredient in the slurry coating adheres to the folded rubber; however, small amounts of dried powder that do not remain on the surface may become airborne. The Kinston plant used Namicote,[8] a slurry containing a zinc stearate antitack agent, until 1996. A slurry containing Acumist[9]—a finely powdered grade of polyethylene—was used in place of zinc stearate from 1996 until the time of the incident.

Figure 4 shows a plan view layout of the rubber compounding process.

In the batchoff machine, the rubber strip first passes through a dip tank containing a slurry of polyethylene powder and water.

Almost all of the powdered antitack ingredient in the slurry coating adheres to the folded rubber; however, small amounts of dried powder that do not remain on the surface may become airborne.

A slurry containing Acumist— a finely powdered grade of polyethylene—was used in place of zinc stearate from 1996 until the time of the incident.

---

[6]The slurry is referred to in the rubber industry as a "slab dip."

[7]Antitack agents are materials designed to reduce adhesion between surfaces.

[8]Namicote is a trade name of Namico, the National Milling & Chemical Co., Inc.

[9]Honeywell International, Inc. (formerly AlliedSignal Inc.), manufactures Acumist.

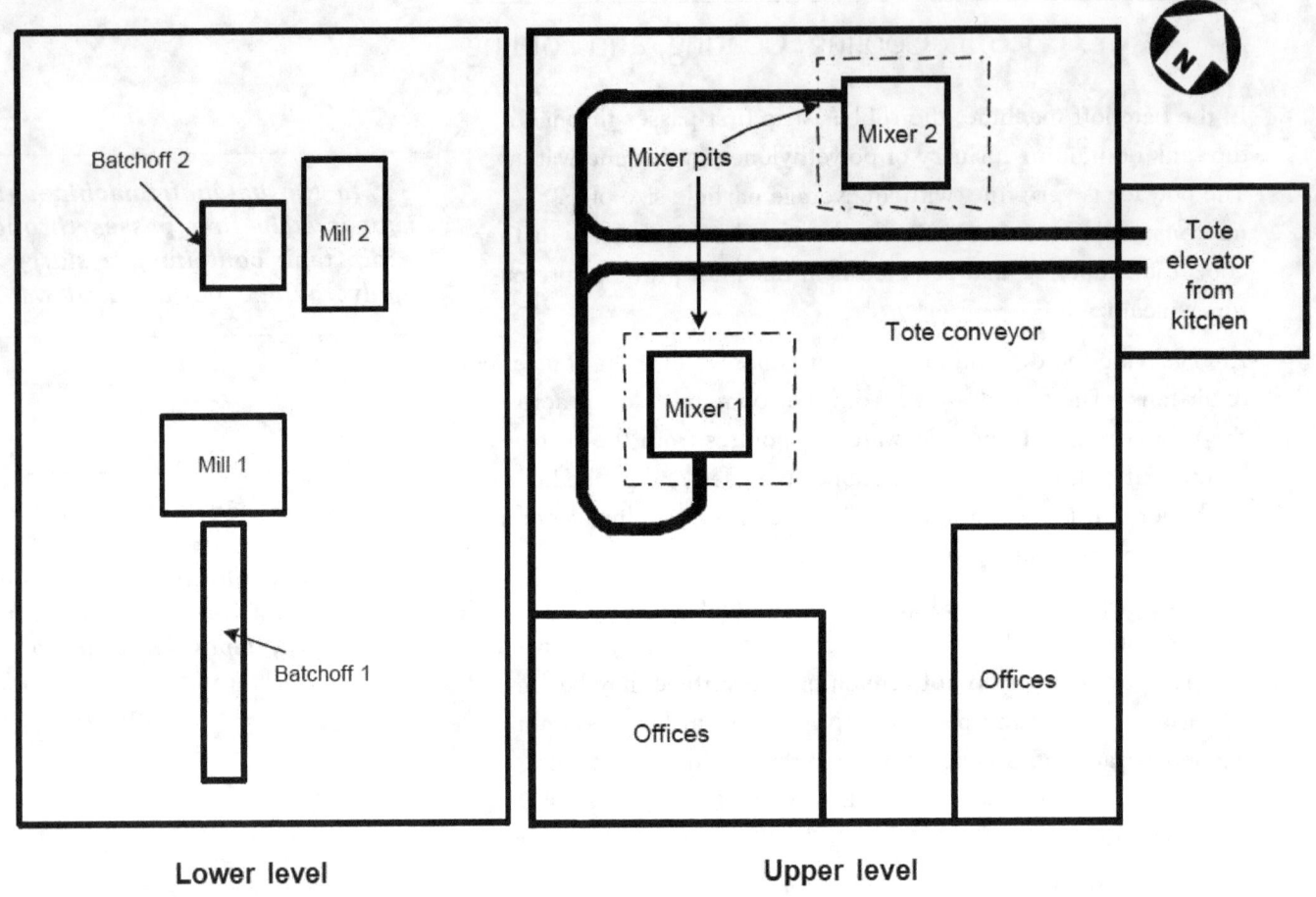

Figure 4. Rubber compounding process plan view layout.

1.6.6 Heating, Ventilating, and Air Conditioning

Air handlers located on the building roof provided comfort air for the milling and batchoff area (Figure 5). They drew air from the room, filtered and heated or cooled it (mixing it with some fresh air), and then returned it. Air from the room generally flowed to the air handlers through ducts (equipped with diffusers) connected directly to the suspended ceiling; however, some ducts

were not so connected and instead drew air from the area above
the ceiling. Because the zone above the suspended ceiling had a
slightly lower pressure than the room it covered, a portion of the
room air was drafted through the ceiling into the open space
above.

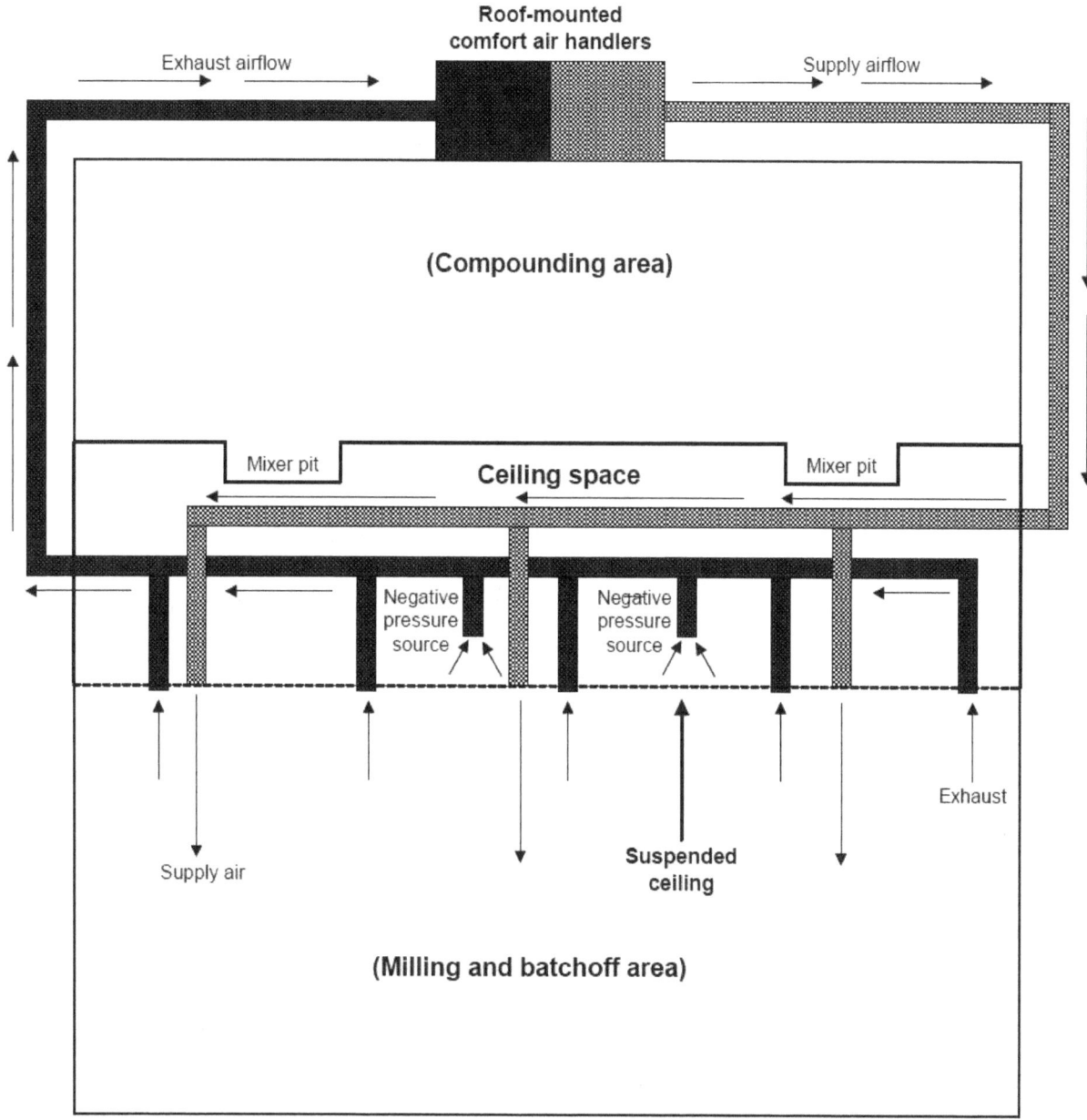

Figure 5. Comfort air system for milling and batchoff area.

The comfort air system for the upper level of the building, where the mixers were located, was not in use. Large exhaust fans on the upper level were sufficient to cool that area of the facility.

1.6.7 Dust Control

West was aware that the compounding process could create dusty conditions. Local exhaust ventilation (LEV) ducts were installed at the mixers and in certain areas of the kitchen, primarily to limit employee exposure to airborne nuisance dusts. The LEV ducts transported dust to outdoor collectors.

West also relied on continuous housekeeping to prevent dust accumulation in work areas. A cleaning staff worked around the clock vacuuming and wiping up dust to minimize visible accumulation on exposed surfaces.

Because West manufactured products for pharmaceutical use, the cleanliness of the facility was a high priority. Management focused on the extent and effectiveness of housekeeping in working areas, and the effort was a matter of facility pride.

Partition walls partially enclosed the batchoff machines to separate them from other areas. Regular housekeeping was conducted around the machines; dehumidifiers/filters associated with the enclosures removed some dust from the air.

Because the zone above the suspended ceiling had a slightly lower pressure than the room it covered, a portion of the room air was drafted through the ceiling into the open space above.

Local exhaust ventilation ducts were installed at the mixers and in certain areas of the kitchen, primarily to limit employee exposure to airborne nuisance dusts.

Because West manufactured products for pharmaceutical use, the cleanliness of the facility was a high priority.

1.7 Description of Incident

. . . Operations on the day of the incident were typical. No one recalled any sights, sounds, or odors that would have indicated a problem.

Interviews conducted by CSB investigators indicate that operations on the day of the incident were typical. No one recalled any sights, sounds, or odors that would have indicated a problem. The explosion occurred abruptly at 1:28 pm on January 29, 2003. Employees throughout the plant heard the explosion, which some described as sounding like "rolling thunder." After seeing the exterior siding blow off the second story of the compounding structure, witnesses outside saw a fireball and a rising smoke cloud.

Inside the facility, employees had varying observations. Those most distant from the compounding area saw lights flickering, and ceiling tiles and debris being blown about. Some workers saw a bright flash and felt either a pressure wave or a vacuum effect that knocked them off their feet. The entire facility was affected to some extent, though explosion damage was most severe in the rubber compounding and milling areas.

A Kinston police officer on patrol less than 1 mile south of the plant noticed smoke above the tree lines that surrounded the facility. He immediately contacted his dispatch to inquire if a controlled burn was taking place at the airport. Seconds later, he observed the smoke rising into a cloud hundreds of feet into the air, and he reported the explosion—which was heard as far as 25 miles away. He immediately proceeded to the scene and began assisting victims out of the facility to safety.

U.S. Army reservists from a quartermaster battalion located next to West in the same business park estimated that they entered the burning building within 3 minutes of the blast and helped at least five employees to safety. National Guard personnel from a nearby armory arrived shortly thereafter; they assisted fire-fighters and other responders by providing additional first aid and stabilizing the injured.

The six people who were killed were working on the ground level of the plant. Three were working near the southeast mill and batchoff machine. The fourth, who died several weeks after the incident, was working at the northeast batchoff. The force of the blast pushed the fifth victim east into the kitchen, and objects on the finishing side of the plant fell onto the sixth person.

The majority of the fatal injuries were either thermal burns or blunt force trauma caused by falling objects or collapsing walls. When police officers entered the facility, one of the victims was pinned under a fallen girder near the end of the batchoff machine. Because of the advancing fire, however, the officers and West employees had to abandon their efforts to rescue this person, who died at the scene.

Immediately after the explosion, many employees were dazed or buried under debris. Responders and other employees equipped with flashlights assisted them out of the plant to triage areas. A

The explosion occurred abruptly at 1:28 pm on January 29.

The entire facility was affected to some extent, though explosion damage was most severe in the rubber compounding and milling areas.

The six people who were killed were working on the ground level of the plant.

The majority of the fatal injuries were either thermal burns or blunt force trauma caused by falling objects or collapsing walls.

The explosion broke feeder lines to the fire sprinkler system, disabling it.

The largest and most persistent fire—which burned for 2 days—developed in the warehouse and involved the large volume of stored baled and strip rubber.

few workers clung to the exposed frame of the building's second story and were rescued by firefighters.

Fires developed throughout the facility. The explosion broke feeder lines to the fire sprinkler system, disabling it. The largest and most persistent fire—which burned for 2 days—developed in the warehouse (Figure 1) and involved the large volume of stored baled and strip rubber. Some of the rubber continued to smolder and flare up for about a week.

1.8 Emergency Response and Facility Damage

1.8.1 Emergency Response

Lenoir County Emergency Management dispatch (9-1-1) received more than 650 radio transmissions and phone calls in the first 2 hours following the explosion. Because early reports suggested that a plane might have crashed, emergency responders immediately went to a level three response, the maximum alert level. The Kinston City Fire Department responded to what it thought was an accident at the airport, and a mass casualty event was declared.[10] After the true nature of the emergency was determined, Kinston immediately lent mutual aid assistance to the primary responder, the North Lenoir Volunteer Fire Department. The County Emergency Management Division established incident command, while the Kinston fire chief handled fire suppression efforts.

Injured victims were moved to the northwest side of the site and assessed before being transported to local hospitals. A landing zone on a grassy area of the grounds was used for air evacuation of the most severely injured victims to burn trauma centers.

---

[10]At this declaration, Emergency Management officials call out additional rescue equipment and implement other emergency response procedures, which include staging response trucks, establishing triage and treatment areas, and arranging for reinforcement personnel.

Other responding parties included:

- Eight Lenoir County volunteer fire departments.

- Fourteen other fire departments (rendering mutual aid).

- Ten EMS providers.

- Medevac helicopters (used to airlift burn victims to trauma centers in Chapel Hill, Raleigh, and Durham).

- Lenoir County Hospital (implementing its disaster plan).

- Kinston Police Department.

- Lenoir County Sheriff's Office (providing communication and site security).

- North Carolina State Highway Patrol (using a helicopter for aerial spotting of fires spreading beyond the facility and aerial reconnaissance for emergency responders).

- North Carolina State Forestry Service units located in Kinston (attacking the grass and woods fires, starting downwind and working back toward the facility).

Local authorities estimated that equipment and supplies valued at more than $250,000 were consumed or damaged during the firefighting efforts.

All exterior sheathing on the compounding structure was destroyed. Masonry block walls were knocked down, the warehouse collapsed, and the building was rendered mostly unusable.

1.8.2 Facility Damage

The explosion and ensuing fire heavily damaged the compounding section of the Kinston facility. Photographs below and in the remaining sections of this report show the extent of damage. All exterior sheathing on the compounding structure was destroyed. Masonry block walls were knocked down, the warehouse collapsed, and the building was rendered mostly unusable (Figures 6 and 7).

Figure 6. Roof of facility, with two-story compounding section in background.

Figure 7. Remains of ACS warehouse viewed from compounding area.

1.8.3 Facility Relocation

Fourteen months after the explosion, West relocated to an available industrial facility several miles south of the destroyed plant. Some equipment that was not used in the compounding process was salvaged from the original plant and is in use at the new location, and much of the workforce was rehired. At present, however, the destroyed facility and the compounding machinery are not in use.

West is not compounding rubber at the new facility. Rubber strips are being produced by contract manufacturers or at other West facilities and are shipped to Kinston for molding.

Fourteen months after the explosion, West relocated to an available industrial facility several miles south of the destroyed plant.

2.1 Fuel for Explosion

Witness statements and photographs submitted by West indicate that the visible accumulation of dust in the milling area was minimal—even around the batchoff machines. Although the cleaning crew continuously cleaned the areas around the equipment, several employees told CSB investigators of a layer of dust on top of the suspended ceiling, above the room where the rolling mills and batchoff machines were located. Accumulation was reported to be widespread but heaviest in the areas directly above these machines.

Accounts from individual witnesses varied. Employee references to dust accumulations of 0.25 inch were common, but other witnesses described heavier accumulations—such as 0.5 inch or more. One individual who had performed a maintenance job above the ceiling in the months prior to the incident recalled seeing as much as 2 inches of powder in some areas. Another person, who had been above the ceiling 2 weeks before the explosion, estimated an accumulation of up to 0.5 inch across 90 percent of the ceiling area. The company investigation concluded that the overall dust accumulation ranged from 0.125 to 0.25 inch in depth.

The area above the ceiling also contained pneumatic conveying lines for the calcined clay and other high-volume noncombustible powders used in the mixers. Because these lines were reported by employees to have leaked on at least one occasion, it is possible that some of the dust accumulation above the ceiling was non-combustible material.

The batchoff machine was a source of fugitive emissions[11] of combustible dust.[12] Fans blew air across the rubber strip to cool and dry it as it passed through the machine. Some portion of the antitack agent was carried on air currents into the room, where it tended to settle on surfaces. The cleaning crew continuously

> *Although the cleaning crew continuously cleaned the areas around the equipment, several employees told CSB investigators of a layer of dust on top of the suspended ceiling . . .*

> *Fans blew air across the rubber strip to cool and dry it as it passed through the [batchoff] machine. Some portion of the antitack agent was carried on air currents into the room, where it tended to settle on surfaces.*

---

[11]Fugitive emissions are those released to the air other than from stacks or vents. Examples include equipment leaks, evaporative processes, and wind-blown disturbances.

[12]The National Fire Protection Association (NFPA) Standard 654 defines combustible dust as any finely divided solid material 420 microns or less in diameter that presents a fire or explosion hazard when dispersed and ignited in air.

wiped and vacuumed the dust from surfaces so that the area was generally free of visible accumulation.

The comfort air system created a slight negative pressure above the suspended ceiling, and room air was pulled into this zone, where conditions were favorable for the settling of dust. West changed out large areas of ceiling tiles from time to time—primarily for aesthetic reasons because they tended to discolor. However, the frequency of replacement was insufficient to address dust accumulation. There was no organized cleaning program for surfaces of beams, conduits, and other features above the ceiling.

CSB investigators recovered a sample of the antitack slurry agent from the dip tank of one of the batchoff machines. It was sent to Safety Consulting Engineers, Inc. (SCE), in Schaumburg, Illinois, where it was dried to a powder under vacuum and tested for combustibility in accordance with American Society for Testing and Materials (ASTM) guidelines. Dispersions of the powder in air were confirmed to be combustible. (See Appendix A for test results.)

Because no other material capable of producing such a large explosion was present or used at the plant, CSB concludes that accumulated polyethylene dust above the ceiling tiles fueled the explosion. Section 2.1.1 presents supporting data for this conclusion. Several other possibilities were investigated and determined to be not credible, as described in Section 2.1.2.

There was no organized cleaning program for surfaces of beams, conduits, and other features above the ceiling.

Dispersions of the [antitack slurry agent] powder in air were confirmed to be combustible.

. . . CSB concludes that accumulated polyethylene dust above the ceiling tiles fueled the explosion.

2.1.1 Polyethylene Dust: The Only Credible Fuel for Explosion

There is general agreement in the scientific literature that a dust explosion requires the following five simultaneous conditions:

- Combustible dust (of sufficiently small particle size)
- An oxidizer (such as air)
- Dispersion of the dust (into air)

- A confined environment (such as a building)

- An ignition source.

These requirements are sometimes represented as a pentagon (Figure 8), similar in concept to the well-known fire triangle.

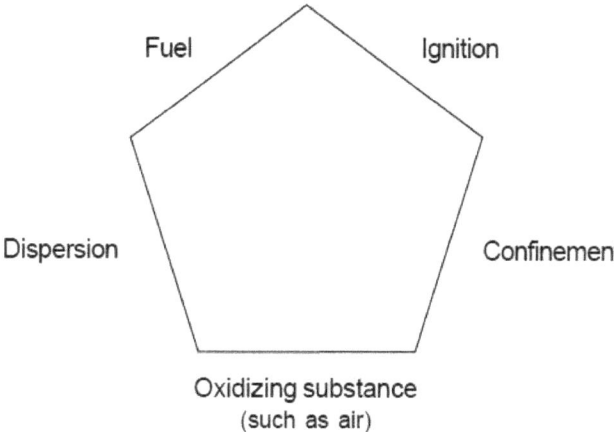

Figure 8. Dust explosion pentagon.

Eckoff (1997) explains that the concentrations of dust in air required to create an explosive mixture are so high that a combustible cloud will appear opaque to an observer at close range. The minimum explosive concentration is typically a thousand or more times higher than that which would cause employee discomfort or hygiene concerns.

During interviews, West employees described no such visible dispersions of dust in the air. Thus, it is not a realistic possibility that explosive concentrations of dust were normally present in production areas of the plant, including the area around the batchoff machines. It is apparent that accumulated polyethylene dust above the ceiling tiles was the only fuel source available for such a large explosion. CSB investigators were unable to conclusively determine what dispersed the dust to create an explosive cloud.

Resting accumulations of combustible dusts are known to be hazardous:

- NFPA Standard 654, *Standard for the Prevention of Fire and Dust Explosions From the Manufacturing, Processing, and Handling of Combustible Particulate Solids* (2000), explains that a 1/32-inch dust accumulation over the floor area of a room, if uniformly suspended, can create a 10-foot-high cloud of optimal explosive concentration. It warns that accumulations may be hazardous when they exceed just 5 percent of the floor area (e.g., on exposed beams and joists).

- The Health and Safety Executive of the United Kingdom warns (HSE, 2003):

  > The most important mitigation measure is maintaining the process building in a clean condition . . . Do not neglect the highest parts of buildings as these are the areas where the finest and most hazardous dust can be found.[13]

2.1.2 Other Fuel Sources Considered

The following potential fuel sources were considered by CSB but determined to be not credible for the reasons given:

- **Flammable liquid:** No flammable liquids were stored in the compounding area, other than a water-alcohol solution used for cleaning that was dispensed from small-volume containers.

- **Natural gas:** The natural gas piping for the facility did not traverse the area of the explosion; the zone through which it passed was essentially undamaged during the event. The surviving witnesses did not report the smell of natural gas odorant prior to the explosion.

---

[13]HSE also specifies a dust accumulation layer that is considered to be hazardous (i.e., 1/84 inch over 100 percent of an area). Although such an accumulation is thinner than the NFPA limit, this amount of dust over an entire floor represents greater total dust mass than the NFPA limit of 1/32 inch over 5 percent of the floor area.

- **Propane cylinders:** Propane in small-volume cylinders was used as a fuel for lift trucks and floor sweepers within all production areas of the West facility. Investigators searched the rubber compounding area in which the explosion occurred, but found no evidence of a failed or leaking cylinder. The warehouse fire following the explosion eventually affected the propane fuel cylinders, causing at least one to explode. However, witnesses reported this explosion to have occurred well after the initial blast, and it was not close to the primary explosion.

- **Other combustible dust:** The majority of the powders used in the West plant were not combustible, such as silicon dioxide, barium sulfate, calcined clay, and titanium dioxide—which were added to the rubber mixers in large quantities. Small quantities of combustible powders, such as sulfur, were added to certain rubber batches. Local exhaust ventilation drew dust emissions from the kitchen and second-floor mixing areas to exterior dust collectors.

CSB investigators recovered samples from the dust collectors for combustibility testing. The samples are very likely representative of general dust in the facility, excluding dust generated at the batchoff process. Although the samples contained fractional amounts of combustible materials, they were determined to be noncombustible in aggregate.

The majority of the powders used in the West plant were not combustible . . . Small quantities of combustible powders, such as sulfur, were added to certain rubber batches.

CSB investigators recovered [representative] samples from the dust collectors for combustibility testing . . . they were determined to be noncombustible in aggregate.

2.2 Center of Explosion

Dust explosions are infrequently a single event; they often comprise sequential explosions that quickly follow each other. The subsequent events—known as secondary explosions—typically occur when the initial pressure wave disperses dust into the air, and the resulting mixture is ignited by the advancing flame front from the earlier event. Because of this phenomenon, it can be difficult to determine the quantity and sequence of explosions.

CSB investigators determined that the January 29 explosion occurred in the compounding section of the plant. Moreover, the location of the highest pressure was determined to be just east of

. . . The location of the highest pressure was determined to be just east of mill #1.

mill #1 (Figure 9). Force vectors derived from observed damage to the building and surrounding equipment indicate that the largest pressure developed in the compounding section and emanated spherically outward (Figure 10). Appendix B describes the damage patterns CSB used to estimate the directions and magnitude of explosive force.

CSB investigators also recovered ceiling tiles from debris in the plant and from surrounding areas.

- Nearly all of the tiles appeared to be burnt and splattered on the top—but not on the bottom, which had faced the room below.

- Some of the fluorescent light fixture pans recovered from the mill #1 area were flattened from above, as if they had been forcefully driven downward to the concrete floor.

These two items of evidence further support the theory that the explosion occurred within the confined space above the suspended ceiling.

Nearly all of the [ceiling] tiles appeared to be burnt and splattered on the top.

Some of the fluorescent light fixture pans . . . were flattened from above, as if they had been forcefully driven downward to the concrete floor.

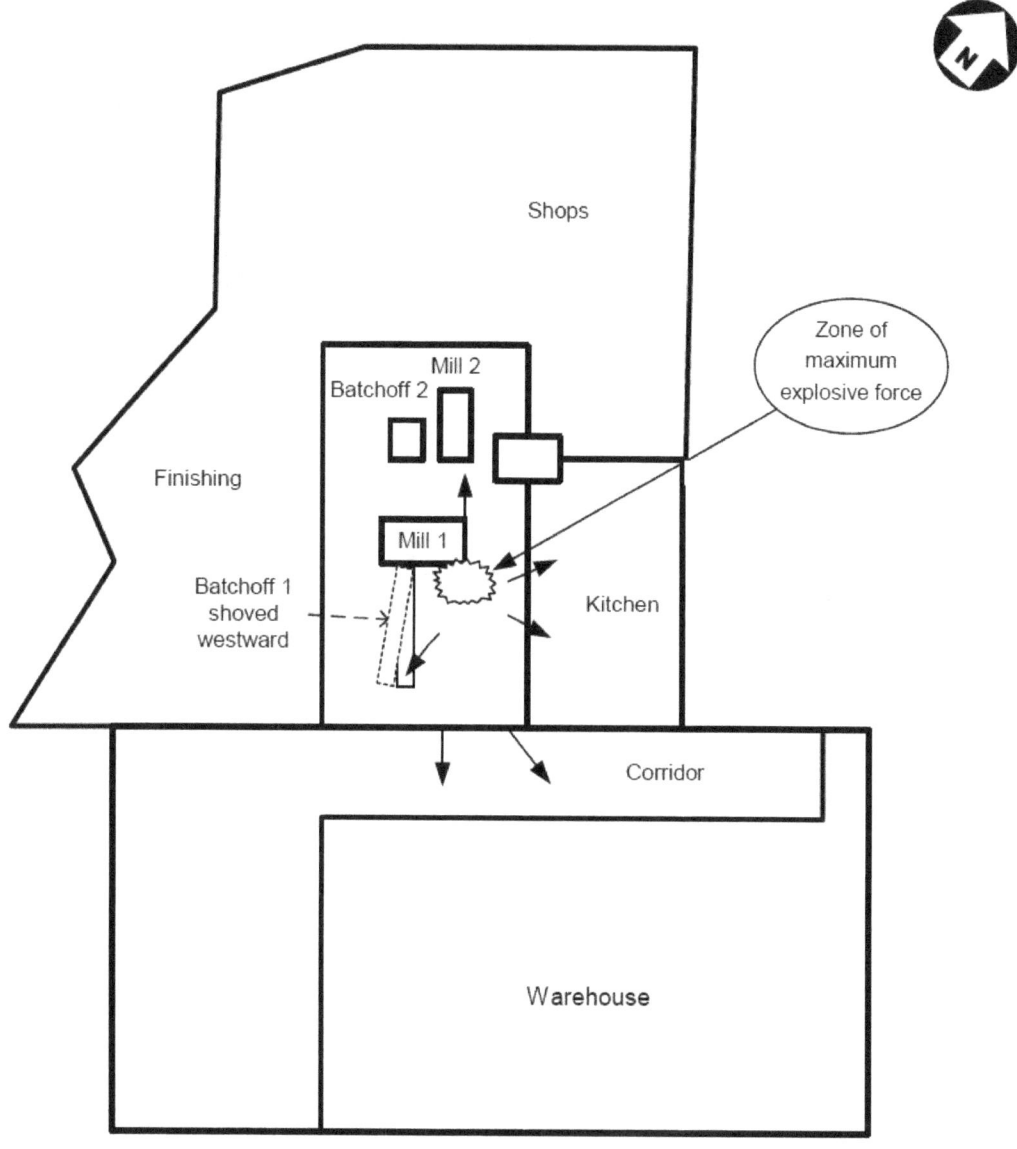

Figure 9. Estimated zone of maximum explosive force.

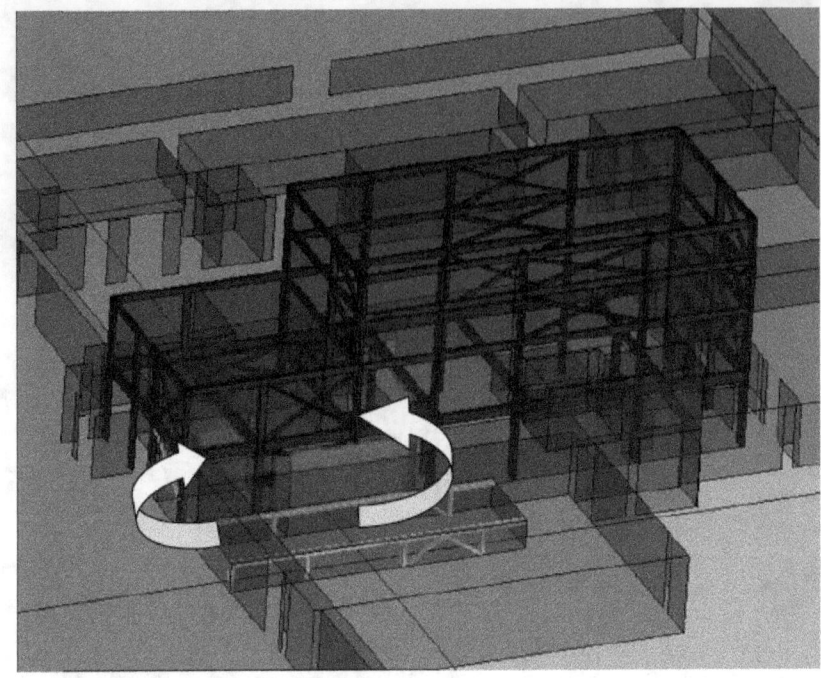

Figure 10. Location of maximum explosive force.

A consultant to CSB used a computational fluid dynamics (CFD) model together with building design details and damage patterns in an attempt to visualize the Kinston accident. However, because such modeling cannot completely account for the complex dynamics of a dust explosion, the CFD model was used only qualitatively, to verify that:

- The explosion occurred on the first floor of the rubber compounding area.

- The explosion pressure from this area was the source of blast damage throughout the facility.

2.3 Acceleration of Fire

The sprinkler system—designed to mitigate incipient fires within the plant—was rendered inoperable from the outset of the incident because the explosion broke feeder lines to the system. Emergency responders reported hearing water freely flowing into the structure.

Rubber and other raw materials were stored in a warehouse southeast of the kitchen and compounding area (Figure 1). The thermal effect from the explosion likely reached this area, igniting incipient fires. Eventually, the entire warehouse was fully engulfed in flames. Heat from the fire caused most of the steel framing to yield and collapse.

West stored mineral oil[14] in two 7,500-gallon plastic tanks located between the kitchen and the warehouse. These tanks failed, spilled their contents, and burned to the ground. The release of combustible liquid further fueled the fire in the warehouse. Two additional but smaller plastic tanks containing mineral oil were located near the warehouse; they, too, failed and contributed fuel for the fire. The concrete masonry retention walls around the tanks failed and did not prevent the burning oil from spreading.

> *The sprinkler system . . . was rendered inoperable from the outset of the incident because the explosion broke feeder lines to the system.*

> *West stored mineral oil in two 7,500-gallon plastic tanks . . . These tanks failed, spilled their contents, and burned to the ground. The release of combustible liquid further fueled the fire in the warehouse.*

2.4 Initiating Event

CSB believes that the accumulation of combustible dust above the suspended ceiling is the most important safety issue in the West incident. Because it is virtually impossible to eliminate all ignition sources from an industrial setting, preventing the accumulation of fuel provides the best protection against fires and explosions.

The extent of damage to the Kinston facility made it extremely difficult to definitively determine the event that dispersed the dust or what ignited it (Figure 11). Investigators focused on the most pertinent hazard—the accumulation of combustible dust—and considered the initiating event as a matter of secondary

> *. . . The accumulation of combustible dust above the suspended ceiling is the most important safety issue in the West incident.*

---

[14]The mineral oil had a flash point greater than 200 degrees Fahrenheit (°F). NFPA 30, *Flammable and Combustible Liquids Code* (1996), classifies such materials as Class IIIB liquids, which do not ignite below the flash point; however, once ignited, they burn vigorously.

importance. CSB was unable to determine whether any of the following theories may have been the actual initiating event:

- Overheating of a batch of rubber and subsequent ignition of the vapors produced by thermal decomposition.

- Ignition of the dust layer by an overheated electrical ballast or light fixture.

- Ignition of the dust layer by an electrical spark from an unidentified electrical fault.

- Unsettling of dust in a cooling air duct for an electric motor and subsequent ignition of the dust by the motor.

Appendix C further discusses these theories.

The extent of damage . . . made it extremely difficult to definitively determine the event that dispersed the dust or what ignited it.

CSB was unable to determine whether any of the following theories may have been the actual initiating event:
- *Overheating of a batch of rubber and subsequent ignition of the vapors . . .*
- *Ignition of the dust layer by an overheated electrical ballast or light fixture.*
- *Ignition of the dust layer by an electrical spark . . .*
- *Unsettling [and ignition] of dust in a cooling air duct for an electric motor . . .*

Figure 11. Extensive damage and debris near mill and batchoff machine #1.

2.5 Engineering

The construction of a new production facility may involve the integration of product and process development with building design. The West corporate engineering department focused on product development. Outside firms conducted detailed process and facility design for the Kinston compounding project, as well as construction.

The West corporate engineering group developed the concept for the new compounding process to be built at Kinston. However, West relied on several engineering contractors for design, planning, and implementation. For example, one firm designed the material handling and mixing systems, while another designed the building and overall facility. The batchoff machines were a common design used in various industries. West purchased the batchoff machines directly from the manufacturers.

West corporate chemists developed the formulations for the rubber and specified the powders to be used in antitack solutions. Zinc stearate is used as an antitack agent in the rubber industry, and West had used it in dry powder form for other purposes—well before the automated rubber compounding system (ACS) was built. However, when West purchased the batchoff machine (which used blown air for drying and cooling), the hazardous properties of zinc stearate with respect to its use in the manufacturing process and building were not fully evaluated.

NFPA 499, *Recommended Practice for the Classification of Combustible Dusts and of Hazardous (Classified) Locations for Electrical Installations in Chemical Process Areas* (1997), identifies zinc stearate as a combustible dust. However, the material safety data sheet (MSDS) for zinc stearate slurry—used by West corporate personnel to evaluate the material as an antitack agent—did not include combustible dust warnings.

Any building that contains a process that produces or uses a material classified as a combustible dust should be designed in accordance with relevant codes and standards. In this case, the 1982 version of NFPA 654, *Standard for the Prevention of Fire and Dust Explosions in the Chemical, Dye, Pharmaceutical, and Plastics Industries*—available when the process was designed—

The West corporate engineering group developed the concept for the new compounding process . . . However, West relied on several engineering contractors for design, planning, and implementation.

. . . When West purchased the batchoff machine (which used blown air for drying and cooling), the hazardous properties of zinc stearate with respect to its use in the manufacturing process and building were not fully evaluated.

. . . [The] MSDS for zinc stearate slurry—used by West corporate personnel to evaluate the material as an antitack agent—did not include combustible dust warnings.

... The 1982 version of NFPA 654 ... available when the process was designed— contained comprehensive guidance on measures to control the hazards of combustible dusts.

West managers relied on the engineering design firms to ensure that the work met all applicable codes and standards, though West itself was positioned to most fully understand the materials and their use in the manufacturing process.

contained comprehensive guidance on measures to control the hazards of combustible dusts.

Although there was no fire code in force in North Carolina in 1985—when the ACS was built—best engineering practice calls for reference to available codes and standards regardless of whether they are adopted by local regulation. West managers relied on the engineering design firms to ensure that the work met all applicable codes and standards, though West itself was positioned to most fully understand the materials and their use in the manufacturing process.

There is no evidence that West engineers were involved in reviewing the potential hazards posed by replacing zinc stearate with polyethylene as the antitack agent. A comprehensive engineering review following development of the new formulation could have served as an opportunity to identify the associated combustible dust hazard and to implement the precautionary measures described in available codes and standards.

West did not conduct a formal project safety review of the ACS process at the time of design. Although formal project safety reviews are widely accepted in industry today, they were not common practice in general manufacturing in 1985—nor were the concepts of process safety as widely known outside the chemical industry as they are today.

For example, West currently makes occasional use of failure modes and effects analysis (FMEA)[15] as a tool for evaluating some processes. Likewise, many manufacturing companies make project management responsible for adhering to internal hazard assessment policies as well as external codes and standards. Today, formal safety reviews are increasingly common during the design, engineering, and construction of processes. Such reviews can help identify the hazards of materials such as combustible dust and alert project management to the need to avoid inappropriate design features for dusty areas (e.g., unsealed suspended ceilings). West was not required by statute or regulation to

---

[15]FMEA is one of the systematic analysis methods recognized by OSHA for process hazard analysis in the chemical process industry (20 CFR 1910.119 (e)).

perform these reviews when the ACS was constructed, nor would it be similarly required to do so today.

2.6 New Material Safety Review

Before new materials are introduced into a manufacturing process or workplace, it is important to review them for hazards and potential safety issues. Reviews of this type typically consider the information contained in MSDSs and in more comprehensive technical and scientific literature.

West has a formal management system in place for conducting new material reviews. Corporate personnel consider potential safety issues before new materials are introduced. Reviews are performed by a committee and approved by the regulatory affairs administrator, quality control chemists, and product group manager. The focus is primarily, but not exclusively, on toxicity issues and U.S. Food and Drug Administration (FDA) requirements.

In 1990, West corporate personnel reviewed Acumist, a fine polyethylene powder,[16] for use in limited quantities as a dusting agent. Several years later, another review was conducted for the use of a slurry containing Acumist in water suspension to replace the zinc stearate slurry as the antitack agent in the batchoff machine. Neither review identified the associated combustible dust hazard.

To understand why the reviews did not identify combustible dust hazards, it is useful to review the company's use of the material as an antitack agent.

The following chronology (pages 44–45) outlines West's history of assessing and using antitack agents (see Appendix E for a timeline):

Before new materials are introduced into a manufacturing process or workplace, it is important to review them for hazards and potential safety issues.

---

[16]This was a micro-fine grade of an average particle size of 12 microns, referred to as "micronized."

Use of Antitack Agents at Kinston Facility

1987

The ACS is first put into operation at West's Kinston facility. Zinc stearate, in a preformulated aqueous slurry called Namicote, is used as the antitack agent for the rubber strips. The MSDS for Namicote does not include dust hazard warnings. According to currently available MSDSs and NFPA standards, zinc stearate in dry powder form is a combustible dust.

1990

West corporate conducts a new material review of Acumist powder for use as a directly applied dust for trials of Teflon-coated rubber stoppers at a St. Petersburg, Florida, manufacturing facility. The 1988 MSDS for Acumist is referenced in this review. The MSDS states:

❖ "Avoid conditions that create high levels of product in the air in a closed room as a dust explosion hazard can exist."

❖ "Sweep up with a minimum of dusting. Remove ignition sources. Keep away from heat or flame."

The MSDS does not refer readers to NFPA 654; however, the section on "Fire and Explosion" hazards states:

❖ "High levels of product in the atmosphere may present a dust explosion hazard. Appropriate precautions should be observed."

West consults a technical data sheet included with the MSDS, "Static Electricity and Fine Particle Size Polyethylene Waxes." The data sheet addresses static electricity and the hazard of using the polyethylene with solvents. It does not mention that the polyethylene powder is, itself, a combustible material. It states that housekeeping is of prime importance but does not explain that accumulations of the powder pose a hazard of dust explosion.

The housekeeping warning in the MSDS may be unclear because it is presented in the context of static electricity hazards.

West intends to use the polyethylene powder as a directly applied dust agent in small quantities and in a manner that is unlikely to result in static electricity or significant fugitive dust emissions.[17]

---

[17]West managers told CSB investigators that they did not consider the hazards outlined in the MSDS and technical data sheet to be relevant to their intended use of the material.

1992

West comes into possession of a revised MSDS for Acumist, dated March 1990. The "Fire and Explosion" section advises users to consult NFPA 654.

The review committee does not refer to the revised MSDS because West is already using the product and the material was previously reviewed. However, the MSDS is transmitted to personnel at the Kinston plant.

1994

West corporate staff directs suppliers to develop formulations to replace the zinc stearate antitack slurry in the batchoff machines with a slurry containing Acumist polyethylene powder. West contracts with Crystal, Inc.–PMC[18] to produce a concentrated water-based paste of polyethylene powder.

Crystal produces an MSDS for the water-based paste, describing it as a benign substance without health or safety risks. The MSDS contains no combustibility warnings, though Crystal understands the end use of the material and is aware that fine polyethylene powder is combustible.

West corporate staff conducts a new material review for the polyethylene paste produced by Crystal, referring to the Crystal MSDS. The review team notes that the polyethylene powder ingredient—Acumist—was reviewed in 1990 and decides not to re-evaluate it. The current review excludes a specific engineering component to consider how using this material as an antitack agent in the batchoff machine rather than as a dusting agent may create different conditions (i.e., the polyethylene is used in greater quantities in the batchoff machine, and there is greater potential to release it into the air.)

1996

The Kinston facility begins using the polyethylene slurry as the antitack agent to coat rubber strips. Kinston employees dilute the paste with water to obtain the desired slurry consistency before adding it to the batchoff dip tank.

---

[18]Crystal, Inc.–PMC is a subsidiary of PMC Group International, Inc., based in Lansdale, Pennsylvania. It manufactures or blends waxes, oils, soaps, and detergents.

As detailed below, the new material reviews West conducted on Acumist as a dusting agent (in 1990) and on a paste containing Acumist as an antitack agent (in 1994) did not identify combustible dust hazards or lead to the mitigation of dust hazards:

- The technical information available at the time the Acumist polyethylene powder was first reviewed for use as a dusting agent contained some hazard warnings regarding combustible dust; however, the warnings were not considered to be relevant in the minor application envisioned.

- The second review failed to identify the dust hazard associated with an antitack slurry containing polyethylene powder. The committee did not review the documentation from the earlier review and considered only the properties of the aqueous paste and the MSDS supplied by Crystal (which contained no combustible dust warnings). The revised 1990 Acumist MSDS—which contained the reference to NFPA 654—was not referred to.

2.7   Previous Incidents

CSB investigators learned that in an earlier maintenance operation involving welding, polyethylene powder in proximity to the batchoff machine had ignited, but the fire self-extinguished. This event demonstrated that the powder was ignitable.

There is no documented investigation of the welding incident. A comprehensive incident investigation, with documentation and sharing of lessons learned, might have led to broader awareness of combustible dust hazards. Given that West went to great lengths to keep working areas clean and free of dust accumulation, it is likely that West also would have cleaned above the ceiling had it understood the hazard posed by settled dust.

3.0 Regulatory Analysis

Fire codes protect the public and property by conveying basic facility safety requirements. Two codes are commonly used in the United States:

- National Fire Codes, published by NFPA.

- International Fire Code (IFC), published by the International Code Council (ICC).

Both sets of codes address the hazards of combustible dusts.

States, localities, and cities typically set minimum fire safety standards by adopting a code or by incorporating one by reference into regulations or administrative requirements. In 1991, North Carolina adopted the Standard Fire Prevention Code, published by the Southern Building Code. In 1994, the Southern Building Code Congress International, Inc., merged with other code organizations to form ICC. In 2000, this council revised IFC, which the State of North Carolina adopted in 2002.

3.1 State Fire Safety Regulations

. . . The State of North Carolina adopted [the International Fire Code] in 2002.

3.1.1 Combustible Dusts

The National Fire Codes and IFC each have a distinct approach to addressing dust hazards:

- The National Fire Codes are written in directive language and are highly prescriptive. Several NFPA standards set out specific minimum technical measures for managing the hazards of agricultural dusts, powdered metals, coal dust, sawdust, and chemical and plastic dusts.

  NFPA 654, *Standard for the Prevention of Fire and Dust Explosions From the Manufacturing, Processing, and Handling of Combustible Particulate Solids* (2000), and its predecessors are pertinent to the situation at West. They specify engineering and construction requirements for dust-tight segregation of hazardous building zones, classification of electrical equipment in dusty areas, and special air conditioning requirements and explosion venting—in addition to recommending management systems for fugitive

NFPA 654 . . . and its predecessors are pertinent to the situation at West.

dust emissions, associated housekeeping, and employee training. The 2000 edition of NFPA 654 requires retroactive application of the requirements for training, management of change, and housekeeping.

Unlike the extensive hazard coverage in various NFPA standards, IFC contains only a single page of text on combustible dust.

- Except for very limited treatment of housekeeping and ignition source precautions, IFC Chapter 13, "Combustible Dust-Producing Operations," does not include specific engineering and management system measures to control combustible dust hazards. Unlike the extensive hazard coverage in various NFPA standards, IFC contains only a single page of text on combustible dust.

Chapter 13 references various NFPA standards for combustible dust hazards. Instead of mandating compliance with these standards, however, IFC "authorizes" the "code official" (the government authority having jurisdiction) to enforce "applicable provisions" of NFPA standards on a case-by-case basis to prevent and control dust hazards. IFC promotes this activity by requiring that a government authority issue an operating permit to facilities that use or generate combustible dust.

Some North Carolina localities require permits for facilities that use or generate combustible dusts; however, Lenoir County does not.

When North Carolina adopted IFC in 2002, it made numerous amendments to the code—including making permits optional for industrial facilities that use or generate combustible dusts. Although local authorities determine whether permits are required, local fire officials are not necessarily involved in determining what protective measures facilities may take to control dust hazards. Some North Carolina localities require permits for facilities that use or generate combustible dusts; however, Lenoir County does not.

3.1.2 Combustible Liquids

IFC addresses the storage of combustible liquids inside structures by incorporating NFPA 30, *Flammable and Combustible Liquids Code* (1996). It recommends that storage tanks be made of steel or some other noncombustible material. Tanks made from combustible material, such as plastic, are allowed by exception for Class IIIB liquids only—provided that the facility owner obtain approval from the local code enforcement authority. For this class of liquids, the building must be equipped with an approved automatic fire extinguishing system; however, safeguards for the control of spillage, such as diking, are not required.

West stored mineral oil—a Class IIIB combustible liquid—in two 7,000-gallon plastic tanks and two 300-gallon plastic tanks located inside the building, near the warehouse (Figure 1). The tanks were surrounded by dikes constructed of concrete masonry units. However, because the tanks were installed before North Carolina adopted IFC, there was no legal requirement for West to seek approval of the local authority.

Although the Kinston facility had a sprinkler system, as required by NFPA 30, it was rendered inoperable due to damage from the explosion. As discussed earlier, the mineral oil tanks released their combustible contents following the initial explosion and fire—at which point, the liquid added additional fuel to the fire in the ACS warehouse.

West stored mineral oil—a Class IIIB combustible liquid—in two 7,000-gallon plastic tanks and two 300-gallon plastic tanks located inside the building . . . However, because the tanks were installed before North Carolina adopted IFC, there was no legal requirement for West to seek approval of the local authority.

3.1.3 Fire Inspectors

Local authorities conduct fire safety inspections of commercial facilities in North Carolina. Inspectors are certified according to State standards set by the North Carolina Code Officials Qualification Board. Inspectors are trained to three levels of competency. Inspection officials told CSB investigators that their familiarity with combustible dust hazards and control measures was limited—even at the third level of competency. Current training programs contain only minimal coverage of dust hazards and control measures.

3.2 Federal and State Occupational Safety and Health Regulations

3.2.1 Combustible Dusts

OSHA promulgated a dust standard for grain-handling facilities in 1987, in response to repeated loss of life from grain elevator explosions. Similarly, the Mine Safety and Health Administration has issued standards for coal dust. Other than these regulations, however, no specific Federal program provides for safety standards to prevent and control the hazards of combustible dusts in industry.

Section 18 of the Occupational Safety and Health Act of 1970 encourages states to develop and operate job safety and health programs. OSHA approves and monitors these state plans. North Carolina is one of 26 states that have adopted a state OSHA plan.

In areas where OSHA does not exercise regulatory authority, states are permitted to adopt their own regulations, with OSHA approval. No specific combustible dust regulations exist in North Carolina beyond those in the Federal standards. Following the explosion, NCOSHA reached a settlement with West for a single violation of the employer's general duty to provide a safe workplace for employees.

NCOSHA inspected the Kinston facility in fall 2002 and cited West for allowing employees to use compressed air hoses to blow dust from their clothing (i.e., as an impact and eye injury hazard). The inspectors were unaware of the existence of combustible dusts in the facility. Moreover, inspectors also told CSB that they had limited understanding of combustible dust hazards beyond sawdust and grain dust.

3.2.2 OSHA Hazard Communication Standard

The OSHA Hazard Communication Standard (HazCom; 29 CFR 1910.1200) requires chemical manufacturers to evaluate chemicals produced or handled in their workplace and to communicate the associated hazards—through MSDSs, labeling, and training—to exposed employees. MSDSs should accurately reflect the basic hazards of chemical products and contain generally applicable precautions and control measures. Manufacturers and distributors must label their products and transmit associated MSDSs to downstream customers.

In addition, the HazCom inspection procedures directive CPL 2-2.38, paragraph (d)(1)(a), states that the hazard determination conducted by chemical manufacturers:

> . . . must consider the potential exposures that may
> occur when downstream employers use the product,
> and address the hazards that may result from that use
> on the label and MSDS prepared for the product.

Employers that are not chemical manufacturers must communicate hazard information to exposed employees using MSDSs, labeling, and training. HazCom also requires any employer using hazardous materials to make MSDSs readily accessible to exposed employees.

Although the Kinston plant had the 1990 MSDS for Acumist, CSB interviews of workers revealed that West's training had not informed them of combustible dust hazards. The system of safety is best served by well-informed workers, who are more likely to identify accumulations of combustible dust in less traveled plant areas and to raise their concerns to management.

As noted above, HazCom requires chemical manufacturers like Crystal to address the downstream hazards of their products. CSB found that Crystal was aware of the end use of the polyethylene slurry it sold to West; and also aware that, when dry, it was a combustible dust. However, the Crystal MSDS for the slurry contained no combustibility warnings and addressed only the potential hazards of the aqueous slurry itself.

Although the Kinston plant had the 1990 MSDS for Acumist, CSB interviews of workers revealed that West's training had not informed them of **combustible dust hazards.**

*. . . **Crystal was aware of the** end use of the polyethylene slurry it sold to West; and also aware that, **when dry, it was a** combustible dust. However, the Crystal MSDS for the slurry contained no combustibility warnings and addressed only the potential hazards of the aqueous slurry itself.*

3.3 Guidance Documents

Beyond U.S. Bureau of Mines information, CSB found little Federal guidance on the hazards of combustible dust. European agencies, such as HSE in the United Kingdom, do publish guidance on combustible dust.

Following the explosion at West, NCOSHA published a brief industry alert on combustible dust.[19] This 2-page document summarizes the hazards of combustible dust explosions; the reader is referred to the National Fire Codes and National Electric Code (NEC; NFPA 70 [2002]) for further information.

As discussed in Section 3.1.1, NFPA 654 (2000) lists several measures for preventing or mitigating dust explosions. Specific elements that apply to the circumstances at West are noted below:

- Separate areas in which combustible dusts are processed or handled from other areas.

- In areas in which combustible dusts are processed or handled, seal dust-tight all penetrations of floors, walls, ceilings, or partitions.

- Seal areas inaccessible to housekeeping to prevent dust entry.[20]

- Equip processes that generate dust with dust collectors.

- Classify areas where a hazardous quantity of dust accumulates or is present in suspension in air in accordance with NEC (NFPA 70; 2002).

- Routinely conduct initial and refresher dust hazard training.

---

[19] This document is available at www.dol.state.nc.us/osha/etta/CombDust.pdf.
[20] Earlier versions of NFPA 654 (1982) advise: "Concealed spaces shall be sealed to prevent dust accumulation." The space above the suspended ceiling in the mill/batchoff area was such a concealed space.

3.4 Combustible Dust: A Hazard Not Readily Apparent

Early in the investigation, it became apparent to CSB investigators that it would have been difficult for an uninformed observer or inspector to identify the combustible dust explosion hazard at the Kinston facility. The hazardous dust had accumulated above the suspended ceiling, out of sight. The working areas were regularly cleaned. Even if inspectors had noticed the dust—without knowing that its source was the antitack slurry at the batchoff, and without knowledge of the properties of the antitack component—it was not obvious that the dust was combustible.

Several safety inspectors visited the facility but did not recognize or identify the hazard. Among these professionals were the following:

- An industrial hygienist hired to evaluate employee inhalation exposure to dusts, who did not include any mention of combustible dusts in his report.

- NCOSHA officials, who inspected the facility 2 months before the explosion but did not observe the dust accumulation.

- Risk insurance carriers, who inspected the facility and pointed out the need to remove dust from sprinkler heads but did not mention combustible dust hazards in their reports.

Early in the investigation, it became apparent to CSB investigators that it would have been difficult for an uninformed observer or inspector to identify the combustible dust explosion hazard at the Kinston facility.

Even if inspectors had noticed the dust—without knowing that its source was the antitack slurry at the batchoff, and without knowledge of the properties of the antitack component—it was not obvious that the dust was combustible.

4.0 Recent Dust Explosions in United States

Accumulations of combustible dust within industrial facilities create the potential for severe dust explosions. The most serious hazards may actually be secondary explosions, which occur when building vibrations or gases produced by a smaller explosion disperse dust on surfaces into the air. The dispersed dust cloud is subsequently ignited by the advancing flame front of the initial explosion or by other ignition sources. Secondary explosions can be devastating because they tend to bring large amounts of dust into involvement.

Five recent dust explosions are briefly described below:

- **Jahn Foundry, Springfield, Massachusetts:** Powdered plastic resin used as a sand binding agent had accumulated on surfaces in the mold fabrication room of a foundry. On February 25, 1999, the shock from an initial explosion in a dust extraction duct dispersed the accumulated resin into the air, setting up secondary explosions. Twelve employees were severely burned; three of these victims later died. The explosion blew out walls of the building and lifted the roof.

- **Ford Motor Company, River Rouge Plant, Dearborn, Michigan:** On February 1, 1999, a natural gas explosion in an idle power boiler at the River Rouge plant disturbed coal dust that had accumulated on surfaces. The result was a large secondary dust explosion. Six workers were killed, and 14 were seriously injured.

- **Rouse Polymerics International Inc., Vicksburg, Mississippi:** On May 16, 2002, a secondary dust explosion occurred at a Rouse recycling facility. Five workers were killed, and at least seven others were injured. The explosion was fueled by accumulated rubber dust generated from the grinding of scrap tires.

- **CTA Acoustics Inc., Corbin, Kentucky:** A February 20, 2003, dust explosion at this automotive insulation manufacturing plant killed seven workers and injured 42 others. CSB is conducting a root cause investigation of this incident.

- **Hayes Lemmerz International, Inc., Huntington, Indiana:** An aluminum dust explosion at an automotive wheel foundry killed one employee and burned two others. The October 29, 2003, explosion destroyed a dust collector, damaged the building, and ignited a fire that burned for 12 hours. CSB is conducting a root cause investigation of this incident.

5.0 Combustible Dust Hazard Study

During the course of several investigations, CSB has identified gaps in the current understanding of dust explosion risks and shortcomings in approaches for preventing dust explosions. As a result, CSB is conducting a study to define the nature and scope of dust explosion risks in industry and to identify initiatives to prevent dust fires and explosions. Such initiatives may include regulatory action, voluntary consensus standards, or other measures that could be taken by industry, labor, government, and other parties.

6.0 Root and Contributing Causes

6.1 Root Causes

1. West Pharmaceutical Services, Inc., did not perform an adequate engineering assessment of the use of powdered zinc stearate and polyethylene as antitack agents in the rubber batchoff process.

2. The company's engineering management systems did not ensure that relevant industrial fire safety standards were consulted.

3. The company's management systems for reviewing MSDSs did not identify combustible dust hazards.

4. The hazard communication program at the Kinston facility did not identify combustible dust hazards or make the workforce aware of such.

6.2 Contributing Cause

The MSDS for polyethylene paste developed by Crystal, Inc.–PMC did not address the end-use hazard of the product.

7.0 Recommendations

1. Revise policies and procedures for new material safety reviews. (2003-07-I-NC-R1) In particular:

   - Use the most recent versions of material safety data sheets (MSDSs) and other technical hazard information.

   - Fully identify the hazardous characteristics of new materials, including relevant physical and chemical properties, to ensure that those characteristics are incorporated into safety practices, as appropriate.

   - Include an engineering element that identifies and addresses the potential safety implications of new materials on manufacturing processes.

2. Develop and implement policies and procedures for safety reviews of engineering projects. (2003-07-I-NC-R2) In particular:

   - Address the hazards of individual materials and equipment—and their effect on entire processes and facilities.

   - Consider hazards during the conceptual design phase, as well as during engineering and construction phases.

   - Cover all phases of the project, including engineering and construction performed by outside firms.

   - Identify and consider applicable codes and standards in the design.

3. Identify West manufacturing facilities that use combustible dusts. Ensure that they incorporate applicable safety precautions described in NFPA 654, *Standard for the Prevention of Fire and Dust Explosions From the Manufacturing, Processing, and Handling of Combustible Particulate Solids.* (2003-07-I-NC-R3). In particular:

   - Ensure that penetrations of partitions, floors, walls, and ceilings are sealed dust-tight.

   - Ensure that spaces inaccessible to housekeeping are sealed to prevent dust accumulation.

4. Improve hazard communication programs so that the hazards of combustible dust are clearly identified and communicated to the workforce. In particular, ensure that the most current MSDSs are in use and that employees receive training on the revised/updated information. (2003-07-I-NC-R4)

5. Communicate the findings and recommendations of this report to the West Pharmaceutical Services, Inc., workforce. (2003-07-I-NC-R5)

North Carolina Department of Labor, Occupational Safety and Health Division (NCOSHA)

Identify the manufacturing industries at risk for combustible dust explosions, and develop and conduct an outreach program on combustible dust hazards. (2003-07-I-NC-R6)

North Carolina Building Code Council

Amend Chapter 13, Section 1304, of the International Fire Code (as adopted by the North Carolina Fire Code) to make compliance with NFPA 654, *Standard for the Prevention of Fire and Dust Explosions From the Manufacturing, Processing, and Handling of Combustible Particulate Solids*, mandatory. (2003-07-I-NC-R7)

North Carolina Code Officials Qualification Board

Incorporate the provisions of NFPA 654, *Standard for the Prevention of Fire and Dust Explosions From the Manufacturing, Processing, and Handling of Combustible Particulate Solids*, into the training program for State and local building and fire code officials. (2003-07-I-NC-R8)

Modify the material safety data sheet for manufactured polyethylene antitack agents to include hazards posed by the end-use of the product. (2003-07-I-NC-R9)

By the

U.S. CHEMICAL SAFETY AND HAZARD INVESTIGATION BOARD

Carolyn W. Merritt
Chair

John S. Bresland
Member

Gerald V. Poje, Ph.D.
Member

Gary Lee Visscher
Member

September 23, 2004

8.0 References

American Society for Testing and Materials (ASTM), 2000. *Standard Test Method for Pressure and Rate of Pressure Rise for Combustible Dusts*, ASTM E1226-00.

ASTM, 1999. *Standard Test Method for Minimum Ignition Energy of a Dust Cloud in Air*, ASTM E2019-99.

Babrauskas, V., 2003. *Ignition Handbook*, Fire Science Publishers.

Cashdollar, K. L., 2000. "Overview of Dust Explosibility Characteristics," *Journal of Loss Prevention in the Process Industries*, Vol. 13.

Eckoff, R. K., 1997. *Dust Explosions in the Process Industries*, Second Edition, Reed Educational & Professional Publishing Ltd.

Gummer, J., and G. A. Lunn, 2003. "Ignitions of Explosive Dust Clouds by Smouldering and Flaming Agglomerates," *Journal of Loss Prevention in the Process Industries*, Vol. 16.

Health and Safety Executive (HSE), 2003. *Safe Handling of Combustible Dusts: Precautions Against Explosions*, United Kingdom.

Kletz, T. A., 2003. *Still Going Wrong: Case Histories of Process Plant Disasters and How They Could Have Been Avoided*, Butterworth-Heinemann.

Lebecki, K., Z. Dyduch, J. Fibich, and J. Sliz, 2003. "Ignition of a Dust Layer by Constant Heat Flux," *Journal of Loss Prevention in the Process Industries*, Vol. 16.

National Fire Protection Association (NFPA), 2002. *National Electric Code*, NFPA 70.

NFPA, 2000. *Standard for the Prevention of Fire and Dust Explosions From the Manufacturing, Processing, and Handling of Combustible Particulate Solids*, NFPA 654.

NFPA, 1997. *Recommended Practice for the Classification of Combustible Dusts and of Hazardous (Classified) Locations for Electrical Installations in Chemical Process Areas*, NFPA 499.

NFPA, 1996. *Flammable and Combustible Liquids Code*, NFPA 30.

State of North Carolina, 2003. *Combustible Dust Poses a Dangerous, Explosive Threat in the Workplace*, NCDOL Industry Alert, North Carolina Department of Labor, www.dol.state.nc.us/osha/etta/CombDust.pdf.

State of North Carolina, 2002. *State Building Code, Fire Prevention Code*, North Carolina Building Code Council and North Carolina Department of Insurance.

Streitwieser, Andrew, Jr., and Clayton H. Heathcock, 1976. *Introduction to Organic Chemistry*, Macmillan, p. 547.

West Pharmaceutical Services, Inc. (West), 2004. *2003 Annual Report*.

APPENDIX A: Test Results

A.1   Explosivity

CSB contracted with Safety Consulting Engineers, Inc. (SCE), of Schaumburg, Illinois, to perform explosivity testing of material samples from the West Kinston facility. Lycopodium[1] dust, a plant-based industry standard, was tested for comparison purposes.

Samples of the antitack agent paste were recovered from the dip tank on the batchoff machine and vacuum dried. The resulting fine polyethylene powder was tested to determine its severity as a dust explosion hazard. Explosion testing was performed according to ASTM E1226-00, *Standard Test Method for Pressure and Rate of Pressure Rise for Combustible Dusts.* The test was conducted in a U.S. Bureau of Mines 20-liter explosibility test chamber.

Explosion severity is defined by the maximum rate of pressure increase reached in the vessel during the deflagration for an optimum dust concentration in air (P_{max}) and by the deflagration index, K_{ST}. This value is defined by the following equation:

$$K_{ST} = (dP/dt)_{max} \cdot V^{1/3}$$

where:

P	=	pressure (bar)	
t	=	time (sec)	
V	=	volume (m³)	
K_{ST}	=	volume, normalized maximum rate of pressure rise (bar m/sec)	

As shown in Table A–1, testing clearly demonstrates that the dried polyethylene powder is an explosion hazard. The potential explosion severity of dusts is commonly classified by the K_{ST} value. The value of 140 bar-m/sec obtained in this test is proximate to that of many finely powdered plastics. It falls into the same explosion severity classification group as coal, flour, and wood dust.

. . . Testing clearly demonstrates that the dried polyethylene powder is an explosion hazard.

---

[1]Lycopodium is the spore of the club moss plant. The spores, which have a mean diameter of about 30 microns, are spherical in overall shape but feature a high degree of roughness and a correspondingly large surface area. Lycopodium is widely used as a standard material for comparison purposes in dust explosion testing and research.

Table A–1
Explosion Severity Test Results

Material Tested	Particle Size (mesh)	Maximum Pressure Output (psig)	Maximum Pressure Rise (psi/sec)	Deflagration Index K_{ST} (bar-m/sec)
Slab dip from batchoff #1	<-200	121	7,480	140
Lycopodium	-200	107	8,375	157

A.2 Minimum Ignition Energy

. . . MIE provides a relative judgment of the ease of igniting a combustible dust cloud.

Minimum ignition energy (MIE) is measured by using a calibrated spark-generating system in a 1.2-liter clear plastic Hartmann tube per ASTM E2019-99, *Standard Test Method for Minimum Ignition Energy of a Dust Cloud in Air.* By this test method, MIE provides a relative judgment of the ease of igniting a combustible dust cloud. ASTM defines MIE as the amount of electrical energy stored in a capacitor that—when released as a high-voltage spark—is just sufficient to ignite the dust cloud at its most easily ignitable concentration in air.

Tests of dried slab dip . . . resulted in an MIE of 15 millijoules—which is roughly equivalent to the energy released from a static discharge (spark) when a person walks across a carpet and touches a doorknob.

Tests of dried slab dip from both batchoff #1 and batchoff #2 resulted in an MIE of 15 millijoules (mJ)—which is roughly equivalent to the energy released from a static discharge (spark) when a person walks across a carpet and touches a doorknob. Therefore, clouds of the material can be considered readily ignitable.

A.3   Dust Layer Ignition

SCE also tested whether an electrical arc might ignite a resting layer of dried polyethylene powder. A layer of dust was placed between clear plexiglass panels, and a very slight airflow (not enough to disturb the standing dust) was passed down the channel. A 120-volt alternating current (AC) spark was induced in the dust layer at the front of the channel.

In several instances, the spark initiated a propagating dust explosion down the channel. This result suggests that a strong electric discharge could in itself ignite and disperse enough dust to create propagating dust from a standing dust layer. Further research is necessary to confirm this theory.

APPENDIX B:
Blast Damage Observations

CSB used observations of beam deflection and other blast damage to determine where the explosion was most concentrated. Among the notable observations are the following:

- The force of the blast displaced batchoff #1—a machine that weighs several tons—several feet to the southwest.

- To the immediate east of this area, the two masonry walls of a hallway used to conduct tours of the facility were blown northeastward into the kitchen. Structural steel in this area was deflected in the same direction.

- To the southeast, masonry walls for an elevator shaft and stairwell were blown southeastward toward the warehouse. Structural steel and cross bracing were deflected in the same direction (Figure B-1).

- The upper-level concrete slab flooring directly over the mill #1 and batchoff #1 areas was heaved upward. The floor to the northwest between the two mixers was also heaved (Figure B-2).

- Structural steel for the wall adjacent to batchoff #1 was deflected to the southwest (Figure B-3).

In examining the damage to structural steel and masonry block walls, CSB determined that the most severe forces—which emanated with a blast pattern of 360°—were on the first level of the plant in the area southeast of mill #1.

Figure B-1. Beam and cross bracing deflected southeastward toward warehouse.

Figure B-2. Uplifted concrete floor in mixer area.

Figure B-3. Southwest wall of compounding area deflected outward.

APPENDIX C: Initiating Events

CSB considered four theories for ignition and dispersion events, as described in Sections C.1 through C.4. However, evidence was insufficient to determine exactly what ignited the dust above the ceiling.

C.1 Deflagration of Vapors Emitted by Decomposing Rubber

Limited evidence obtained during the investigation supports the possibility that an overheated batch of rubber may have been involved in initiating the explosion. An employee working in the area of batchoff #1 recalls that the batch of rubber that descended from the mixer just prior to the explosion appeared to be evolving shimmering heat waves. The MSDS for the main rubber component in the batch includes a warning that the material may decompose at elevated temperatures and generate flammable vapors. A control failure at the mixer could cause a batch of rubber to overheat.

If the temperature of the rubber rises to the onset of vulcanization, the viscosity of the batch increases. At a constant mixing speed, an increase in viscosity is accompanied by a corresponding increase in mixer torque—which, in turn, is likely to further increase the rubber temperature, accelerating the rate of vulcanization. In short, the temperature of the batch of rubber can run away in the event of a control failure. However, it is not possible to determine if this is what actually occurred because temperature control data for the final batches were lost in the explosion.

Witnesses testified that some batches produced at the Kinston plant over the years exhibited signs of vulcanization and overheating, with some reports that the rubber smoldered or ignited in the drop bucket. Witnesses also stated that sizable static discharges were prevalent around the milling machine. A static spark could ignite vapors if they evolved from the rubber, causing a localized deflagration.[1]

> . . . *The temperature of the batch of rubber can run away in the event of a control failure. However, it is not possible to determine if this is what actually occurred because temperature control data for the final batches were lost in the explosion.*

---

[1]A deflagration is an explosion that moves at a speed less than the speed of sound. Most industrial explosions are classified as deflagrations.

The drop bucket is mounted just below the suspended ceiling. The turbulence created by a deflagration could disturb and ignite the accumulated polyethylene dust above and set off secondary explosions. However, West technical personnel state that the particular grade of rubber being produced at the time of the explosion had not ignited in the past. West also points out that automatic process controls on the mixer are set to drop the rubber to the bucket at a temperature 100°F below the typical vulcanization temperature.

Subsequent to the explosion at West, a fire occurred on a rolling mill at a Michelin rubber preparation facility in Star, South Carolina. The compounding equipment Michelin uses to prepare rubber batches is similar to the equipment at West. Mixers compound the rubber, which is dropped to a rolling mill. Michelin advised CSB that its investigation attributed the incident to a faulty thermocouple measurement that caused the temperature control in the mixer to fail. The batch of rubber overheated to the point of decomposition. When it dropped to the mill and was exposed to oxygen in the air, evolving vapors ignited, creating a flash fire. Employees were injured, but none of the injuries were life threatening.

In another incident, a rubber fire occurred at a Bridgestone tire plant in Graniteville, South Carolina. This plant also uses similar compounding equipment. A rubber strip fell off rollers and accumulated on the floor instead of passing through the water dip tank on the batchoff machine. After a few moments, the rubber ignited and there was a sizeable fire. Bridgestone advised CSB that it attributed ignition of the rubber to the fact that the cooling process was interrupted when the rubber failed to enter the dip tank.

CSB investigators were unable to find any residual rubber near mill #1 at the West facility, even though the witness reported that a batch had been dropped just prior to the explosion. His observations may have been inaccurate (testimony was taken months after the event and followed an extensive recovery from burn injuries), or the rubber may have been consumed in the fire. No other individuals working in the area of mill #1 and its batchoff machine survived the incident.

C.2 Ignition of Dust by Overheated Electrical Ballast or Fixture

Standard 2- by 4-foot fluorescent fixtures,[2] similar to those typically found in office environments, provided lighting for the mill and batchoff area. The fixtures were not rated for use near combustible dust. They consisted of metal pans with tubular fluorescent bulbs and ballasts to supply the necessary voltage. The lights were installed such that the "lens" of the fixture was flush with the suspended ceiling face. The pan with the ballast on top protruded into the space above the suspended ceiling.

Dust layers on the top surface of the light fixtures created an insulating effect. The dust may have caused heat to accumulate in the lighting ballasts. In turn, an overheated ballast may have ignited the dust. If the event was sufficiently energetic, a small dust cloud may have been lofted and ignited, leading to secondary dust explosions. Alternatively, a localized fire above a light fixture—ignited by an overheated, but not failed, ballast—may have generated enough turbulence to set off a chain of dust explosions.

The comfort air system drew a portion of its air from above the ceiling and returned it to the room below. None of the employees interviewed by CSB recalled seeing or smelling smoke prior to the explosion, this scenario would have had to progress fairly quickly for the employees not to have noticed a fire in progress. Comfort air pulled from the area above the ceiling and returned to the working spaces would have retained the odor of smoke.

Dust layers on the top surface of the light fixtures created an insulating effect . . . [and] dust may have caused heat to accumulate in the lighting ballasts.

Alternatively, a localized fire above a light fixture . . . may have generated enough turbulence to set off a chain of dust explosions.

None of the employees interviewed by CSB recalled seeing or smelling smoke prior to the explosion . . .

C.3 Ignition of Dust by Electrical Spark

The fixtures, electrical wiring, and fittings in the zone above the suspended ceiling of the mill/batchoff area were not rated for atmospheres containing combustible dust. NFPA 499, *Recommended Practice for the Classification of Combustible Dusts and of Hazardous (Classified) Locations for Electrical Installations in Chemical Process Areas* (1997), provides guidance on electrical classification where combustible dusts are involved.

---

[2] Per NEC (NFPA 70), the fixtures were not suitable for use in areas with combustible dust. NEC was in force in North Carolina when the ACS was built.

An electrical spark from a malfunctioning lighting fixture or wiring component or an unsealed connection may have ignited the dust layer above the ceiling.

Polyethylene is an NFPA Group II, Class G, combustible dust. Because of the accumulation of combustible dust in most areas above the ceiling at most times, this zone would be classified under the code.[3] At a minimum, electrical equipment would be required to be dust-tight. However, West used general-purpose wiring, junction boxes, and fixtures. An electrical spark from a malfunctioning lighting fixture or wiring component or an unsealed connection may have ignited the dust layer above the ceiling.

C.4 Ignition of Dust in Motor Cooling Duct

The West internal investigation concluded that a small dust explosion in an air duct . . . initiated the larger explosion.

The West internal investigation concluded that a small dust explosion in an air duct that supplied fresh cooling air to the electric motors for mill #2 initiated the larger explosion. This section of duct was above the suspended ceiling. It was distended from internal pressure and partly split open at its crimped edges. Splatter inside the duct was consistent with the residue from dust explosions. Splatter of combustible dust was also found inside the electric motors to which the ducts were attached, including on the brushes.

Other portions of the duct traversed the area above the ceiling tiles and were under negative pressure. Although fresh air from outdoors flowed through the duct, dust could have entered it through a worn canvas coupling.

. . . Portions of the duct traversed the area above the ceiling tiles and were under negative pressure. Although fresh air from outdoors flowed through the duct, dust could have entered it through a worn canvas coupling.

---

[3]According to NEC (NFPA 70) 500.5, Class II, Division 2, locations include those where combustible dust accumulations on, in, or in the vicinity of the electrical equipment may be sufficient to interfere with the safe dissipation of heat from electrical equipment or may be ignitable by abnormal operation or failure of electrical equipment.

APPENDIX D: Logic Diagrams

The CSB investigation team used a combination of two analytical approaches to determine the root causes of this incident:

- First, the available information on the case (i.e., witness testimony, field observations, facts from records, etc.) was placed on a timeline with causal factors.

- Second, the team organized the known causes of the event into a cause map (i.e., a modified fault tree wherein the known and presumed causes are shown but the unproven potential causes are not).

LOGIC TREE

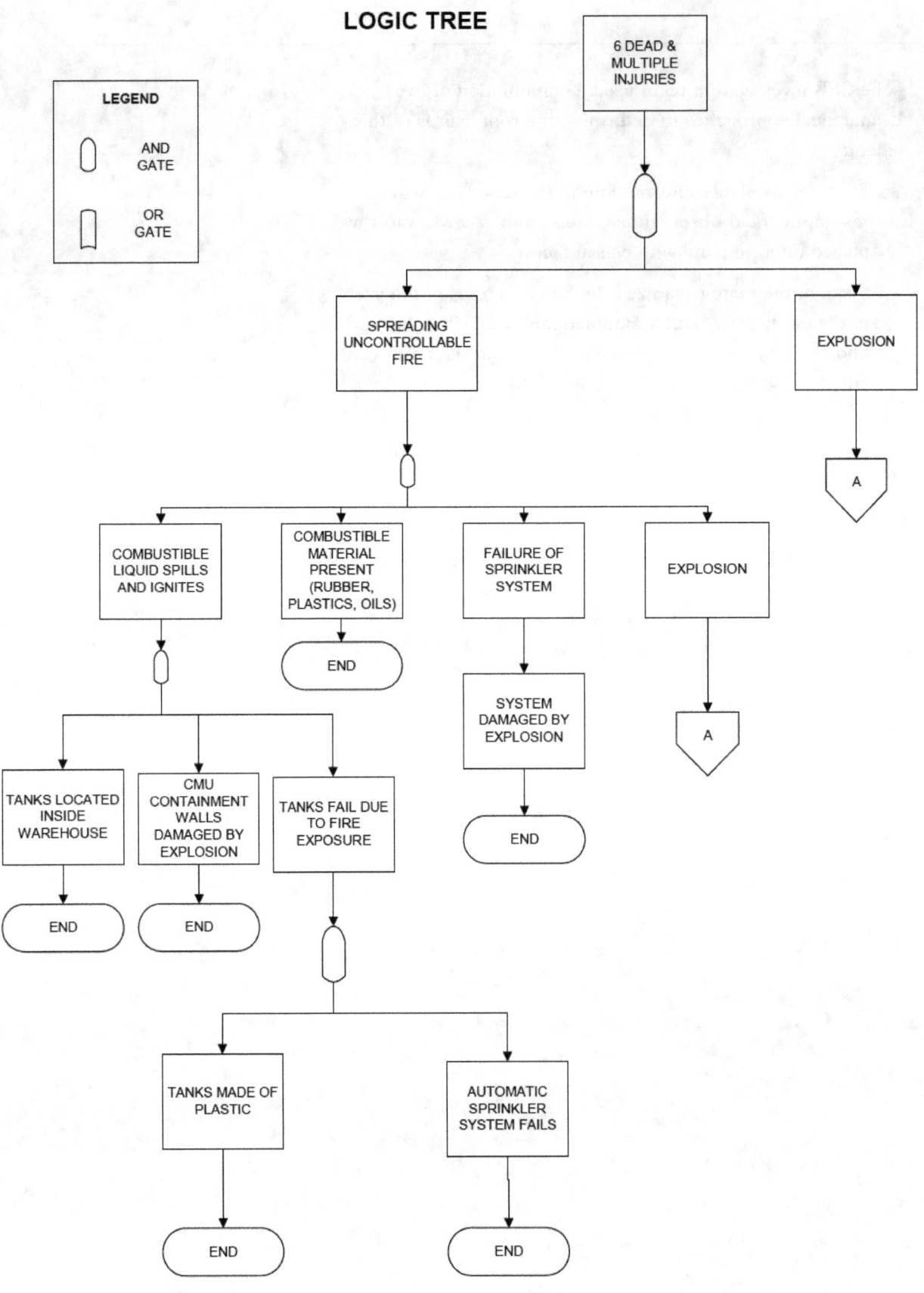

LOGIC
SUB-TREE
A

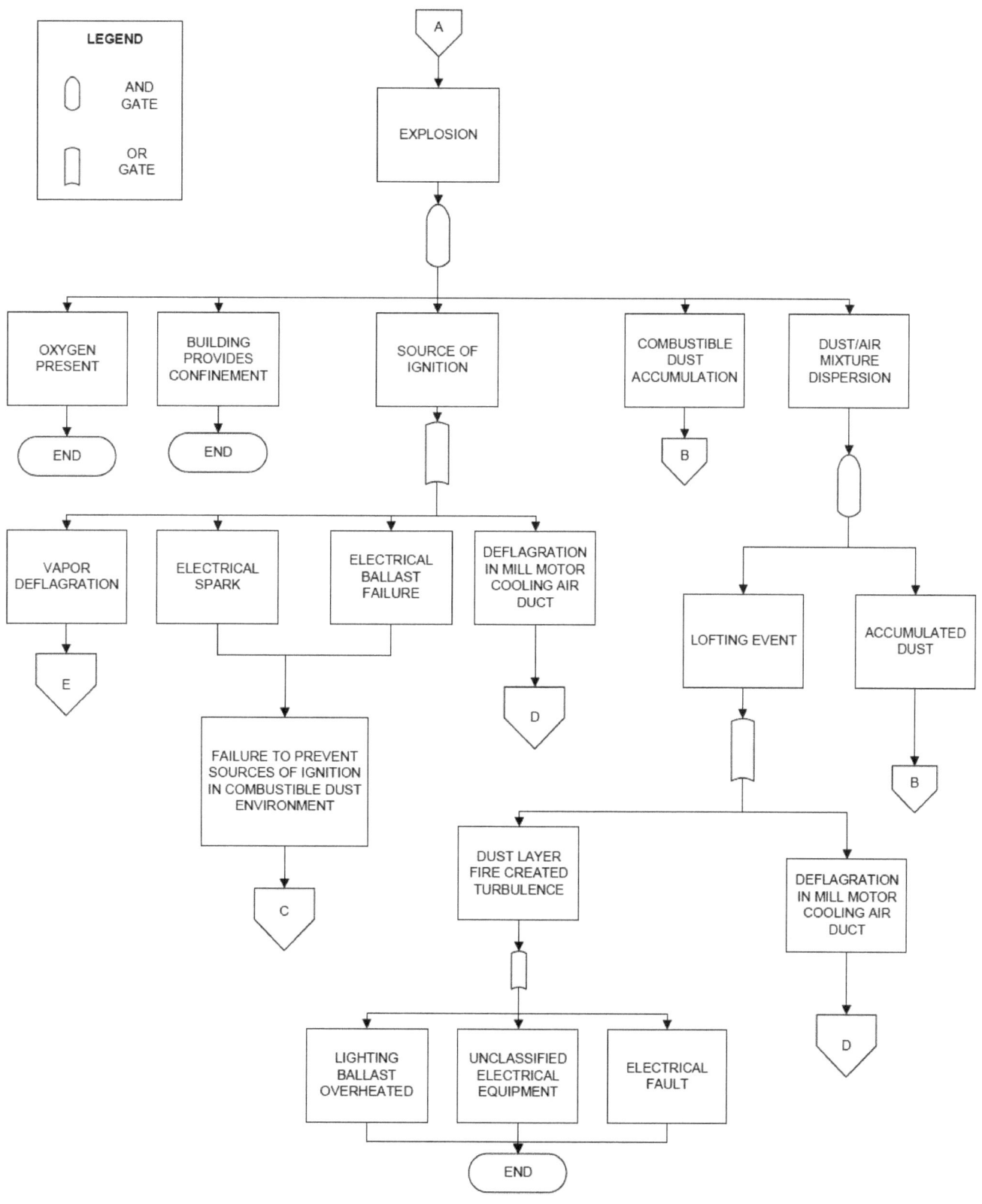

LOGIC SUB-TREE B

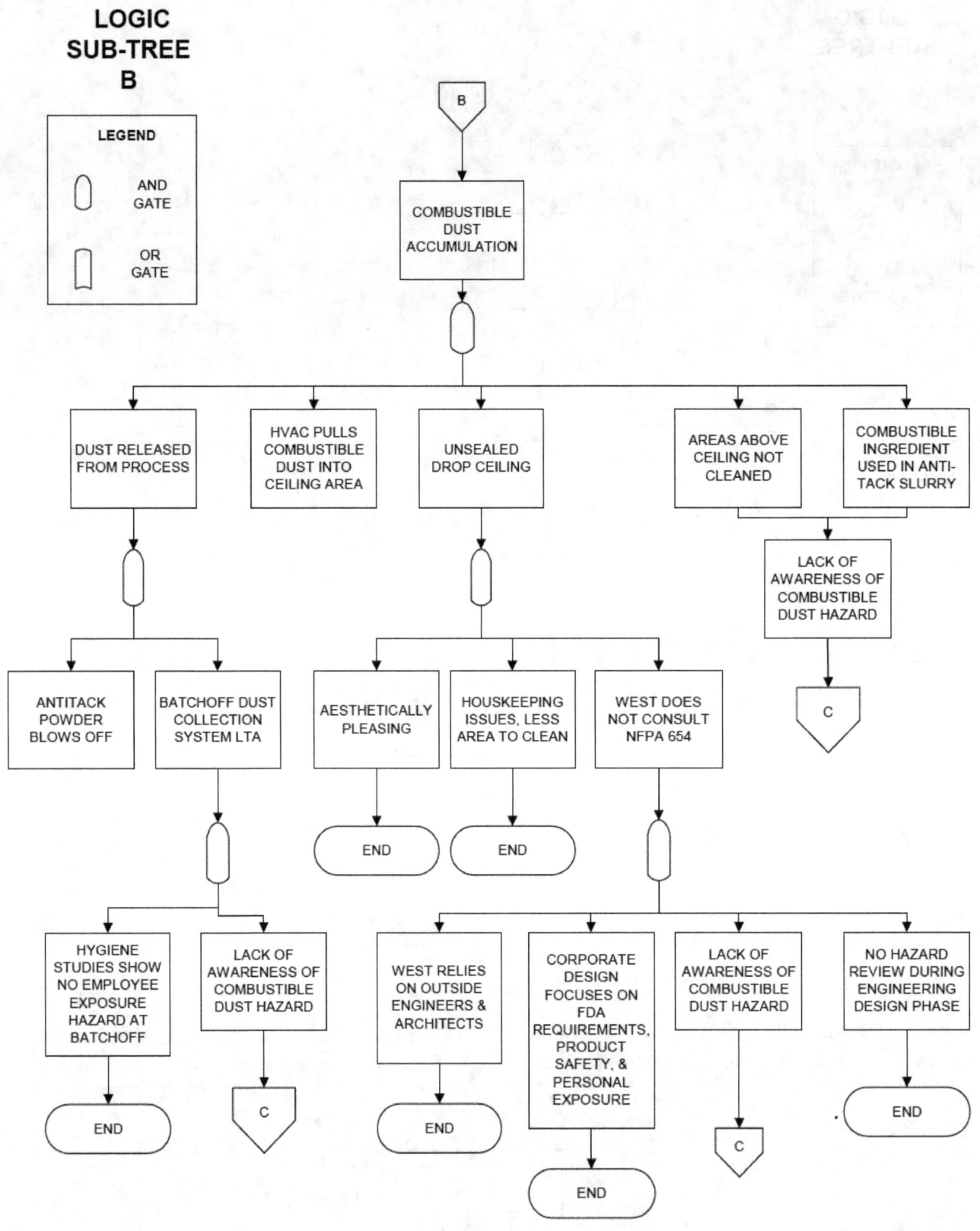

LOGIC
SUB-TREE
C

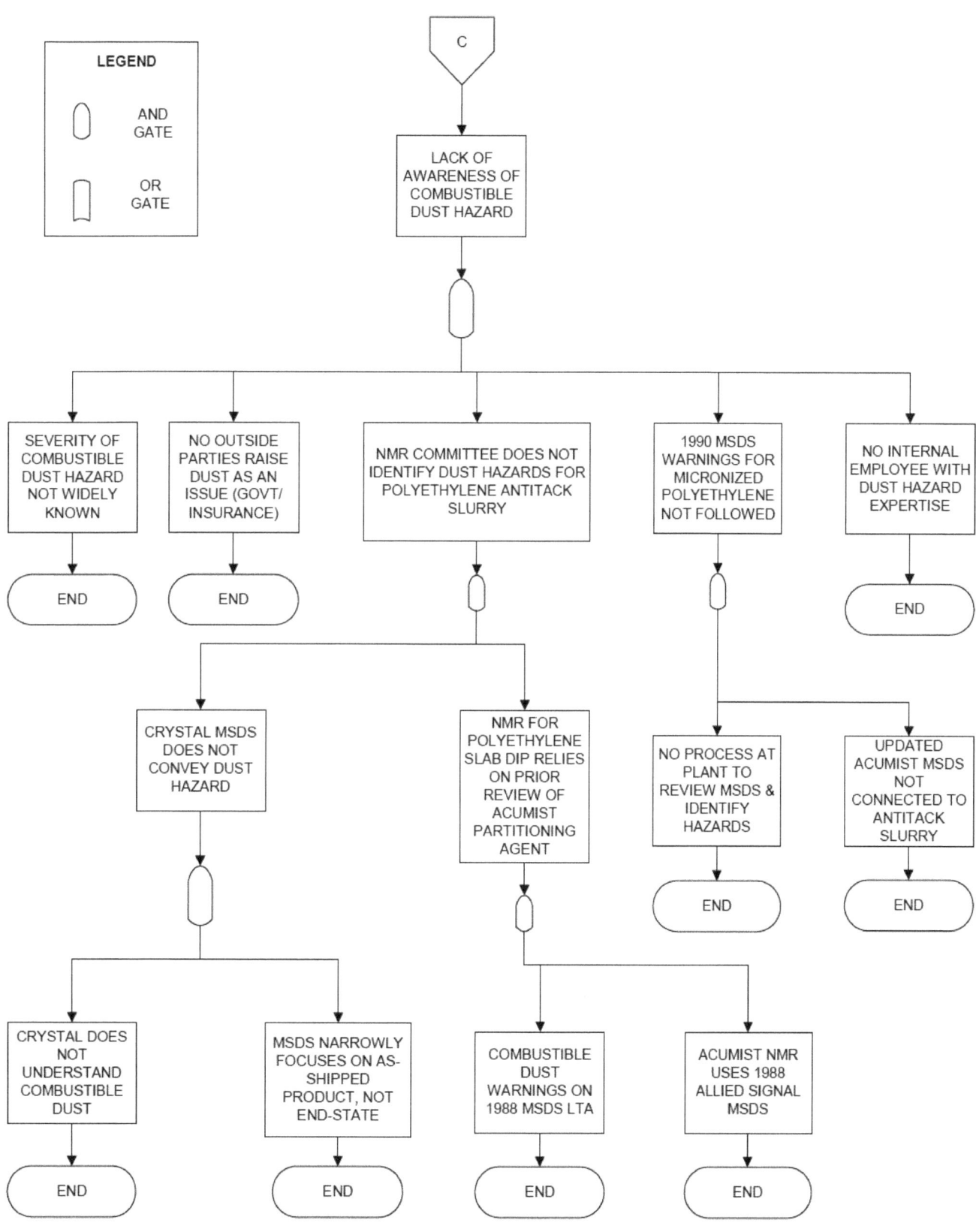

**LOGIC
SUB-TREE
D**

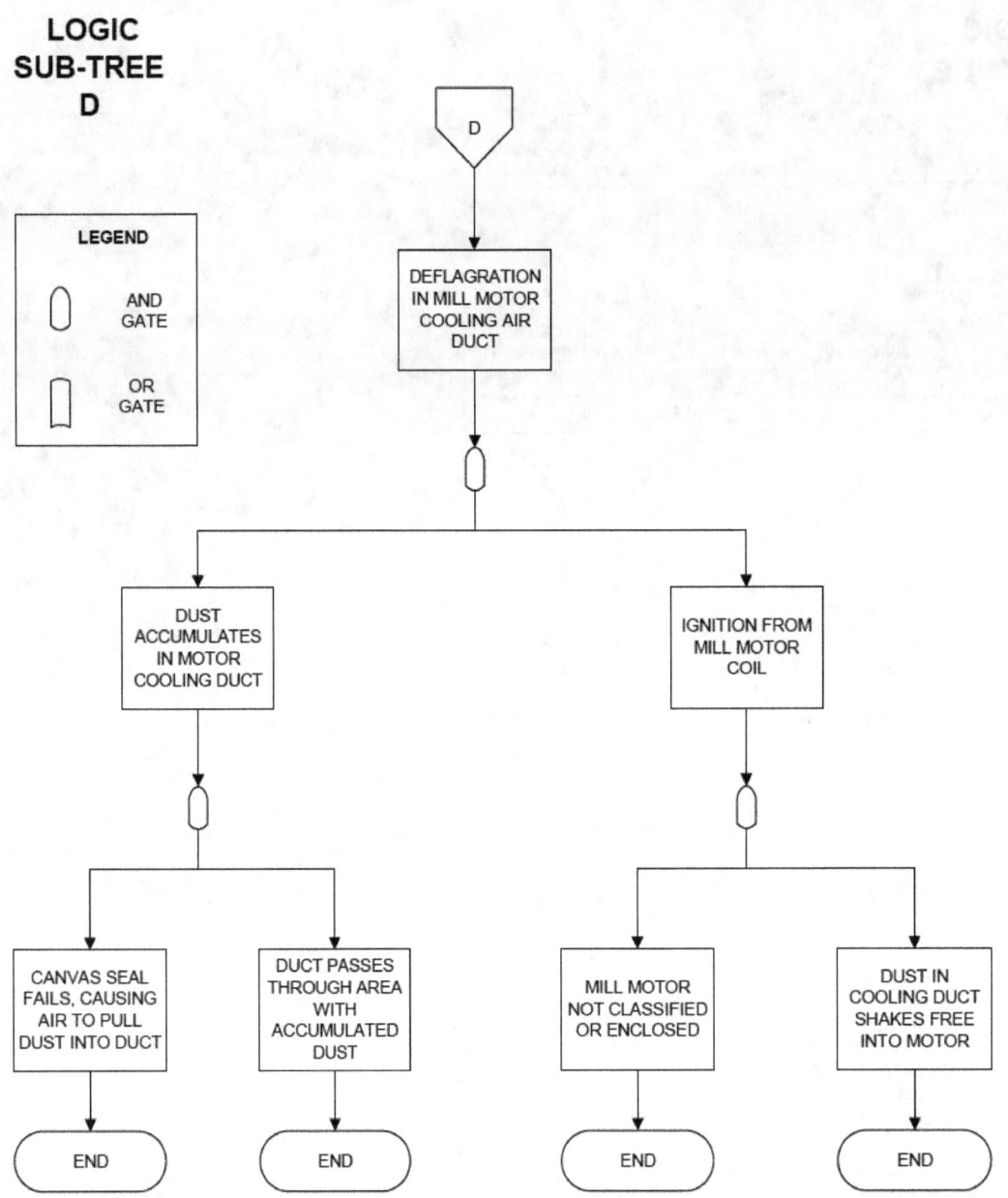

LEGEND

⬭ AND GATE

⬮ OR GATE

D

DEFLAGRATION IN MILL MOTOR COOLING AIR DUCT

DUST ACCUMULATES IN MOTOR COOLING DUCT

IGNITION FROM MILL MOTOR COIL

CANVAS SEAL FAILS, CAUSING AIR TO PULL DUST INTO DUCT

DUCT PASSES THROUGH AREA WITH ACCUMULATED DUST

MILL MOTOR NOT CLASSIFIED OR ENCLOSED

DUST IN COOLING DUCT SHAKES FREE INTO MOTOR

END

END

END

END

LOGIC SUB-TREE E

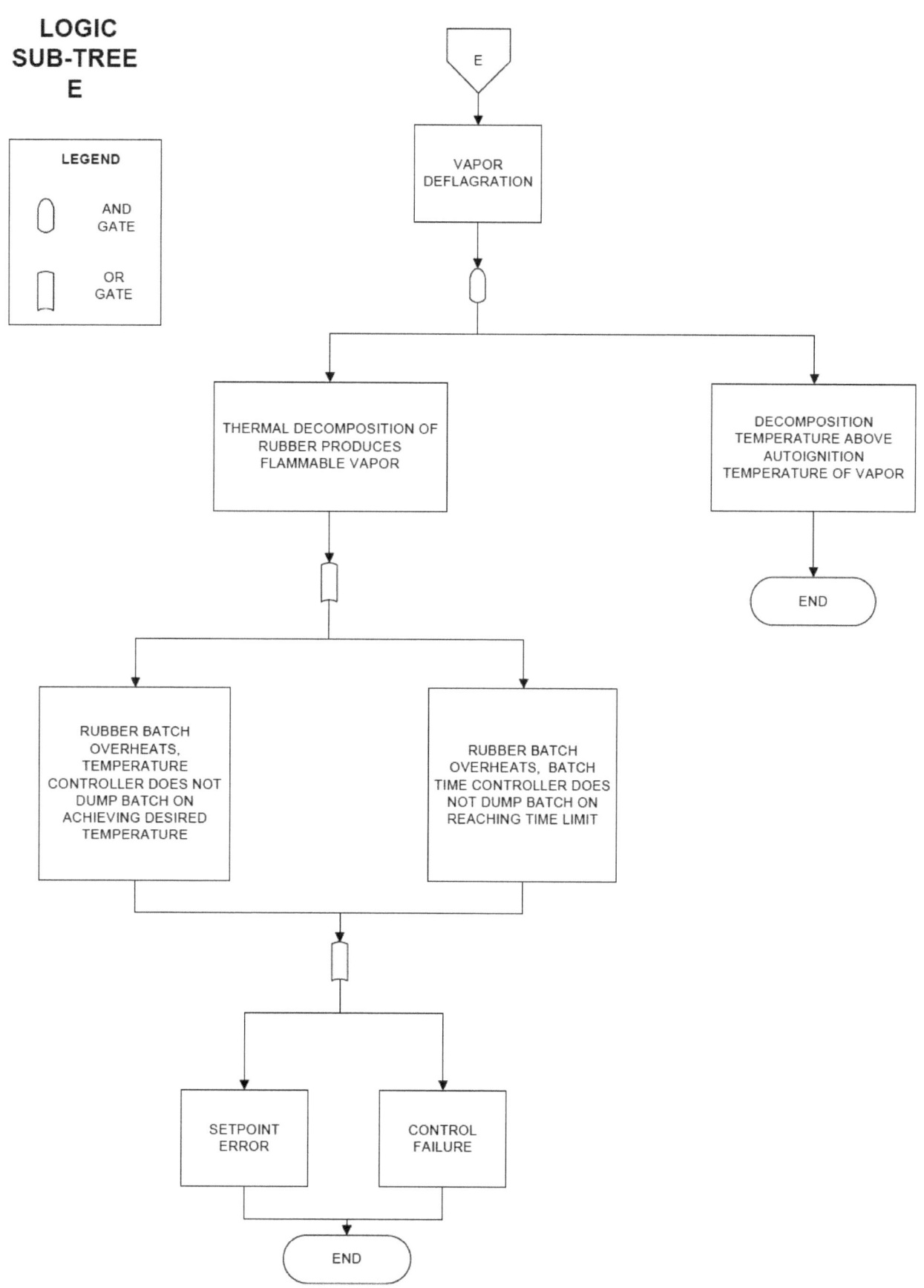

LEGEND

◯ AND GATE

◻ OR GATE

E

VAPOR DEFLAGRATION

THERMAL DECOMPOSITION OF RUBBER PRODUCES FLAMMABLE VAPOR

DECOMPOSITION TEMPERATURE ABOVE AUTOIGNITION TEMPERATURE OF VAPOR

END

RUBBER BATCH OVERHEATS, TEMPERATURE CONTROLLER DOES NOT DUMP BATCH ON ACHIEVING DESIRED TEMPERATURE

RUBBER BATCH OVERHEATS, BATCH TIME CONTROLLER DOES NOT DUMP BATCH ON REACHING TIME LIMIT

SETPOINT ERROR

CONTROL FAILURE

END

APPENDIX E: Timeline

1923   West company founded.

1975   Kinston facility commences production.

1984–1986   West develops concept for new automated rubber compounding system (ACS).

                  Outside engineering firm performs detailed design for ACS process and equipment.

                  Another outside engineering firm designs addition to the Kinston plant structure to accommodate ACS.

1985   West procures batchoff machines from vendor.

1987   Rubber compounding production commences using zinc stearate slurry as antitack agent.

1988   1988 version of MSDS for Acumist is published.

1990   New version of MSDS for Acumist is published.

                  West uses 1988 MSDS to evaluate Acumist as dusting agent for trial run of stoppers to be conducted at St. Petersburg plant.

1993   West works with Namico, which develops antitack formulation using Acumist (as specified by West) as replacement for zinc stearate.

1994   Insurance audits note some dust on fire sprinkler heads, but do not identify type of dust or combustible dust hazard.

                  West enters contract with Crystal, Inc.–PMC to purchase water-based Acumist paste.

                  West uses Crystal MSDS to evaluate Acumist-based paste as replacement for zinc stearate slurry.

                  West ships Acumist powder to Crystal for preparation of test batch of water-based paste.

1996	Crystal begins shipping water-based Acumist paste to West.
	Improved dust collection system is installed in kitchen and mixer areas.
prior to 2001	Spark from welding on batchoff machine contacts dried powder from antitack slurry used in batchoff. Powder on floor briefly ignites and produces small flame that self-extinguishes.
2002	New fluorescent lights are installed in mill area, and some ceiling tiles are replaced.
2003	(January) Ceiling tiles are partially replaced; dust accumulation above ceiling is observed and later estimated to be 0.25 inch in some areas. Dust accumulation is observed over estimated 90 percent of ceiling in mill/batchoff area.
	Dust explosion (January 29).

www.ingramcontent.com/pod-product-compliance
Lightning Source LLC
Chambersburg PA
CBHW081554170526
45166CB00009B/2692